D0010727

RETHINKING SCIENCE AS A CAREER

Perceptions and Realities in the Physical Sciences

SHEILA TOBIAS
DARYL E. CHUBIN
KEVIN AYLESWORTH

W. Stevenson Bacon, Series Editor

An occasional paper on neglected problems in science education

Published by Research Corporation
A foundation for the advancement of science

Dedicated to

Alan Fechter, formerly of the Office of Science and Technology Personnel, National Research Council, National Academy of Sciences, and

To the late and sorely missed Betty Vetter, Director for thirty-one productive years of the Commission on Professionals in Science and Technology,

Who paved our way.

CONTENTS

RESEARCH CORPORATION
101 North Wilmot Road, Suite 250
Tucson, Arizona 85711-3332

Copyright 1995 by Research Corporation

Library of Congress Catalog Card Number 95-68940
ISBN 0-9633504-3-9

Special Thanks

To Stephen T. Abedon, then a graduate student, now on the faculty of Ohio State University, for insisting that the issue of jobs in science belongs on the education reform agenda.

And for providing mailing lists, access to scientists, or directly distributing our various questionnaires, our special thanks to:

Colston Chandler, University of New Mexico
Anthony Starace, University of Nebraska
Edward Langer, Colorado College
Sheila Browne, Mount Holyoke College
Gary Crawley, Michigan State University
Wayne Wolsey, Macalester College
William Titus, Carleton College
Jim Clovis, Rohm and Haas Company
David Barnett, Pfizer Inc.
Brian Gifford, Schlumberger-Doll
Walter Grimes and Sheri Simon, Miles Laboratories
Beverly Hartline, CEBAF

Introduction

In an era in which public support for scientific employment and inquiry are at low ebbs, it is particularly appropriate that Research Corporation, one of the first U.S. foundations and the only one wholly devoted to the advancement of science, publish this appraisal of career opportunities.

Research Corporation was established in 1912 by F. G. Cottrell as an expression of faith in progress and in new knowledge by a dedicated academic scientist and his peers. That story is briefly summarized on page 147, but what bears repeating here is that, long before government became the patron of research, the scientific community itself found resources for financing inquiries and making useful results widely available to the public. Research Corporation, chartered to "provide means for research and experimentation," and "to make inventions and patent rights more available and effective," was one embodiment of its efforts.

It is in that same spirit of independence and with the hope that scientific progress can be maintained that Research Corporation offers this analysis of a difficult problem: how to bring into balance in the post-cold-war period the supply of, and demand for, scientifically-trained professionals. Although the views expressed in this paper are those of the authors, the foundation believes their work will contribute to the current dialogue that too often centers on research cutbacks and other negatives, and too seldom examines the opportunities for scientists in the nonacademic sectors of society.

Research Corporation believes that a rededication of education to the cause of scientific literacy is very much in order; that K-12 and undergraduate science must be extended to all students. Contrary to much prevailing opinion, we also believe that support must be extended for the worthwhile research of talented teacher-scientists and for fundamental inquiry, and that the insights of science must be brought to bear on government legislative and policymaking processes. And, along with the authors of this paper, we agree that a broader training for candidates for advanced degrees might help stimulate demand for their services.

The requirements of the society which largely educates, sustains, and employs scientists must be taken into account in reformulating research and education. Thus, Congressman George Brown, former chairman of the House Committee on Science, rightly called for a new "social compact," while others—less informed as to the need for basic science as a spur for technology—have called for an increased emphasis on research useful to industry. In such a political climate, it is possible that future careers will require that scientists employ new skills and—at the very least—show a new readiness to communicate to the general public the importance of their work.

It is generally agreed that science as a way of knowing can be a sound foundation for a variety of careers; training for a number of opportunities that can use the skills of the scientist while rewarding creativity, autonomy, problem-solving, industriousness, and the yearning for knowledge.

The authors of this book also maintain the obverse: that the nation could use a broad spectrum of professionals whose preparation includes a sound education in science. Such a grounding would help talented young people bring a scientific orientation and some knowledge of how scientists function to the work place, be it government, industry or education, engineering, manufacturing or marketing.

At the same time, it is vital that we not waste scientifically-trained professionals, recent Ph.D.s, and others who are currently un- or underemployed. It would be both foolish and tragic if—given the wide spectrum of economic, environmental, and societal problems that confront us—we fail to put to good use the best minds available.

John P. Schaefer
President
Research Corporation

Tucson, Arizona
July 1, 1995

PROLOGUE

How will our nation grow the scientists it needs?
How will our scientists get the work they've trained for?
And dare we leave these matters to chance?

THERE, on the front page of the *Washington Post* for Christmas 1994, was "American Science: Losing Its Cutting Edge?" the first of three articles on why the nation should worry about careers in science. A picture of Nobel laureate physicist Leon Lederman at the blackboard overlooked the first installment, "Scientific Ranks Outpace Funds."[1] But the nub of the story was captured in a quote from Bruce Alberts, president of the National Academy of Sciences (NAS): "There's always going to be an oversupply of scientists. My own view is that the system has to be competitive. Getting government funding is a privilege. The stiffer the competition, the better the chance that only the best are getting grants." In fact, Bruce Alberts said much more. In his full statement he warned:

> We are presently making life so difficult for our outstanding young scientists that the future of the enterprise is immensely compromised. And once a country loses leadership in an area—whether scientific or industrial—regaining it is expensive and problematic. It would be shortsighted if we failed to make whatever investments are required to meet our important national goals."[2]

Viewed historically, the problems facing U.S. science are those of our society: an imposing deficit that is shrinking discretionary funding; the end of the cold war which has refocused spending for national security; and a robust science work force that can no longer expand. All this cannot help but frustrate the career plans of young scientists and slow our technological progress. As the twentieth century wanes, science is in search of a mantra, a rationale, even a job corps program.

We've reached this agonizing state by training new scientists at an average increase exceeding 4 percent annually since 1977. Since 1987

---

[1] Boyce Rensberger, "Scientific Ranks Outpace Funds," *Washington Post* (Dec. 25, 1994): pp. A1, A20. The data and quotes below are drawn from this article.

[2] The first four sentences in this quotation appeared in the *Washington Post* (cited above). Alberts provided the authors with the full text of the statement.

alone, the science work force has grown at three times the rate of the general labor supply. Temporary positions for postdoctoral scientists have grown even faster (over 5 percent per year since 1989), and those who hold them are being called "the migrant workers of today's high-tech society."[3] To compound the hiring squeeze, the 1990 Immigration Reform Act resulted in a tripling of job-based visas, with scientists representing nearly one-third of the total. In 1979, two of every three postdocs were U.S.-born; in 1992, the ratio was about one to one. During that period the total cadre of postdocs grew from 18,000 to 33,000.[4]

This convergence of events—slackened demand for a still-growing supply of scientists, government budget-cutting, and industry downsizing—has stressed the research and development system as we know it. While all sectors now recognize the need to adapt, prescriptions vary as to how to take the lead and who should take it.[5] In the near term, getting "leaner" has meant getting "meaner."

This book is an analysis of three of the themes noted above: the supply of scientists (a diverse pool of professionals); the privilege of doing science (especially, but not exclusively, research); and the reverence of American science for competition (a value that has ensured U.S. preeminence in science and technology for a half-century). We will argue that it is not just the responsibility of government, but also that of industry, universities, and the science community itself to act on behalf of science, given the crucial role of science to society's well-being. If ensuring utilization of human resources for science is in the nation's best interest, then the employment of well-trained people cannot be an afterthought of scientific and technical investigations. Scientists are part of the lifeblood of a democratic society that rewards those who make contributions to our economic and cultural growth. That *should* be front-page news; for if the attraction of a career in science fades—as the young scientists we queried for this book suggest—so will America's cutting edge.[6]

It is only fair to assert the authors' premises: first, that the market for scientists is no monolith but shaped by economic sector, region of the country, industry, and other factors; second, that the market is not free. If it were, the federal government would not fund graduate education

---

[3] Paul Sotrelis, quoted by Rensberger in "Scientific Ranks."

[4] Ibid.

[5] See *Science in the National Interest* published by the Office of Science and Technology Policy of the Clinton-Gore administration in fall 1994 and intended to launch a national discussion among university, industry, and government sectors. Two of the authors attended the first of a series of regional meetings on Feb. 7, 1995 at MIT.

[6] See Daryl E. Chubin, "Front-page Science: Positive Effects of Negative Images?" *BioScience* 43, no. 5 (May 1993): pp. 334-336.

through fellowships, traineeships, and loans, and indirectly support graduates through research assistantships paid through faculty grants. For better or worse, the government shapes the market by underwriting the supply of scientists and engineers. The third premise is that, if U.S. science and the universities which act as the caretakers of supply, lack a coherent plan for maintaining careers in science, economic turbulence and changes in priorities will inevitably buffet the science community like a cork in an uncertain sea. A mismatch of supply and demand for highly-trained personnel may be a cyclical phenomenon. But a chronic downturn in demand with rising unemployment of Ph.D. mathematicians, physicists, and chemists suggests something more systemic or structural (see chapters 1 and 2 for further discussion).[7] Either way, unemployment means, in the most aggregated and deceptively faceless way, underutilization by our society of needed specialists.

Once we begin to reveal faces, as we do throughout this book, the problem takes on another dimension. There are human beings out there who trained for work in science. If that work doesn't exist or is not adequately supported, society and the science community as a whole will pay the penalty for wasted training, opportunities foreclosed, and productivity forgone. Not long ago, *Science* editor Daniel Koshland opined that "to be a scientist involves extensive training, an insatiable curiosity, and a job."[8] It is in the interests of extending accurate information about jobs for scientists, sharpening perceptions about science as a career, and devising strategies for those who either train or employ physical scientists that this study has been undertaken.[9]

About this Book

This book will explore career issues not simply in the aggregate and by means of statistics, but rather through a "purposive" (nonrandom) sampling of certain populations within science selected for querying because of their probable interest in the issues.[10] In addition, we were able to solicit opinions and experiences via the Internet and the Young

---

[7] The distinction between cyclical and structural causes of the current slackening of demand first surfaced in an article by N. Richard Werthamer, "The Employment Problem—Cyclical or Structural?" *APS Issues* 2 (Mar. 1993): pp. 17-18.

[8] Daniel E. Koshland, Jr. "Where the Grass is Rougher and Greener," *Science* 257 (Sept. 18, 1992): p. 1607.

[9] While careers in science include disciplines other than physical science, this study and its conclusions focus on careers and perceptions of the job market in the physical sciences—physics, chemistry, geology, geophysics, astronomy, and astrophysics.

[10] We recognize one cannot *prove* anything by purposive sampling, and that one cannot derive from it totally reliable estimates. This kind of sampling, however, uncovers otherwise obscure problems and solutions—in this case, attitudes and coping mechanisms.

Scientists' Network.[11] We designed questionnaires to gather impressions along with information from selected target groups of informants: academic scientists and industrial research scientists in midcareer; young scientists looking for work (all or mostly Ph.D.s); and B.A. and B.S. graduates in physics (mostly male) and chemistry (mostly female); representing people who have found traditional and nontraditional ways to use their scientific training. From their responses to direct questions and from their self-reports and comments, we hope to put a human face on the situation as it currently exists, to map out problems along with possibilities, and to suggest ways in which higher education, the federal government, and the science community itself can develop different strategies for projecting and preparing human resources in science for the twenty-first century.

Chapter 1 outlines the scope of the career problem: the sudden and apparently unexpected unemployment and underemployment of physical scientists that began around 1989 and seems to be worsening. We travel back to the incorrectly predicted "shortfall" and explore the reasons (in the government's mode of data collection and interpretation, and in some missed signals) it never materialized. Whether the current downturn is cyclical or structural deserves consideration, and while the authors weigh in on the side of the structural, we do not believe that retrenchment, or so-called academic birth control, is a solution.

In chapter 2 we turn to a description of the traditional expectations of science as a career, noting that there have always been exceptions to these traditions but that the perceptions are more backward-looking than the reality. Chapter 3 investigates how traditional expectations measure up to current realities by presenting summaries of our questionnaire responses from midcareer academic and industrial scientists. In chapter 4 we analyze a sizeable response from an applicant pool of Ph.D. scientists who were actively searching for academic jobs in physics, chemistry, astronomy, and geoscience in 1992-93.

Chapters 5 and 6 offer part of our answer to the questions of what to do and who should do it. We propose, with examples from some new programs, that the *supply* of science-trained professionals be restructured, by which we mean made more versatile and more employable in tomorrow's world. If, as some policy advisers and analysts maintain,

---

[11] The Young Scientists' Network was founded in 1990 by one of our coauthors, Kevin Aylesworth, then a physics postdoc at the Naval Research Laboratory. Frustrated with his and his agemates' inability to land university or industry jobs in physics, Aylesworth sent out a rallying call—where else but on Internet—to young scientists everywhere to create a network to exchange information and job-hunting experience, post jobs, and challenge the then still-official view that there was a "shortfall" of scientists. When, in 1992, Aylesworth and Zachary Levine, a YSN member, were elected to the American Physics Society Council, *Science* reported it as a "shake-up" of the physics establishment. *Science* 262 (Oct. 1, 1993): p. 24.

the greatest challenges to America's research community in the coming years will involve technology transfer and the solution of downstream as well as upstream research problems, then undergraduate and graduate technical education may have to change.[12] We are not alone in thinking about new kinds of training for new kinds of jobs. Some scientists, such as physicists Marvin Goldberger and John Armstrong and chemist Truman Schwartz, are already calling for a broadening of the perspectives and of the experiences of the students they teach.[13]

In chapter 7 we elaborate on the argument that undergirds our recommendations: Properly understood and managed, a supply of differently-trained science professionals will stimulate a demand for their services. Restructuring supply, then, is a necessary (but not sufficient) condition for improving the job prospects of science professionals. Restructuring *demand* should also be an explicit policy of those who care about and are responsible for the future of science and scientists in America. Chapter 7 will conclude with a discussion of how the private and public sectors can mitigate supply and demand imbalances and alter the character of the technical work force.

It should be clear from this outline that we bring to our interpretation of the material some strongly-held views: that much as all professionals like to believe they are in control of their destiny, preparing for a career in science today requires multiple skills and the ability to adjust to shifts in demand and emerging opportunities more than ever before. Because of this, we believe the new generation of physical scientists cannot be created only in the image of the old. That is a prescription for obsolescence and betrayal. Those who train them must be willing to chart a course for their charges even if there is no accurate road map. Those who direct funds to the support of science should see that support in terms of two related purposes: first, to provide the nation with the human capital it requires, and second, to offer scientists the job security and career satisfaction they deserve.

No nation can afford to abandon its young, particularly its talented young. How then to balance supply and sustain demand for scientifically trained professionals? This book will try to answer that question.

---

[12] John A. Alic, Lewis M. Branscomb, Harvey Brooks, Ashton B. Carter, and Gerald L. Epstein, introduction to *Beyond Spinoff: Military and Commercial Technologies in a Changing World* (Boston, Mass.: Harvard Business School Press, 1992).

[13] Marvin Goldberger is former president of Caltech and currently dean of science at the University of California, San Diego. John Armstrong is vice president for research and development at IBM, retired, and Truman Schwartz is on the faculty in chemistry at Macalester College. They have all communicated this sentiment to the authors. See the chap. 5 summary of John Armstrong's talk at the University of Virginia, "What is a Science or Engineering Ph.D. For?"

1

The Job Market in Science

NEW PROBLEMS, OLD PARADIGMS

*Our investment in science speaks volumes about
what our country values and what our country
wants to be.*

—Donna Shalala, Secretary of Health and Human Services[1]

FIFTY years ago this spring, Vannevar Bush, science adviser to President Roosevelt during the whole of World War II, delivered to his new president, Harry Truman, a set of prescriptions for postwar science.[2] Bush was concerned, in the immediate aftermath of WWII, with a future deficit or shortfall of science workers due to wartime career interruptions. In *Science the Endless Frontier*, he paved the way for *two* of the *three* necessary elements of a healthy science infrastructure: federal support for both research and graduate training. His genius was to marry these two by directing funding to university professors to use in part to apprentice the young. So long as the National Science Foundation, NASA, the Departments of Defense, Agriculture, and Energy, and the National Institutes of Health (on the government side), and technology-intensive industries (on the commercial side), grew in mission and size, the third element, sustaining demand for science-trained professionals, did in fact take care of itself.

Evidence for the durability of a supply-oriented point of view is provided by Harvey Brooks, adviser to presidents and Congress alike, writing about supply and demand for scientists nearly twenty-five years later.[3]

---

[1] Donna Shalala, "From Analysis to Action" (opening address at the convocation on undergraduate education of the National Academy of Sciences, Washington, D.C., Apr. 1995).

[2] Vannevar Bush, *Science the Endless Frontier: A Report to the President* (Washington, D.C.: USGPO, 1945), reprinted by the NSF, 1960. See another interpretation of Bush's thinking in Deborah Shapley and Rustum Roy, *Lost at the Frontier: U.S. Science and Technology Policy Adrift* (Philadelphia, Pa.: ISI Press, 1985).

[3] Harvey Brooks, *The Government of Science* (Cambridge, Mass.: MIT Press, 1968), p. 196.

> The rate of incorporation of technical people into our [econo-
> my] is limited primarily by supply rather than demand and this
> will continue to be so. . . . Scientific and engineering manpower
> availability [alone] acts as a spur to development, rather than
> the economy exerting a pull on the manpower supply.

Even if Brooks' view was true in 1968, it is certainly not today. Given the recent decline in job prospects for scientists and the long-term economic and political uncertainties for science, there is little hope that supply by itself will create demand. Rather, the nation must begin to give the same attention to the demand side of the science manpower equation that Vannevar Bush commanded to create a supply.[4] Otherwise, supply will wither, with the least accomplished dropping out first (or, depending on the decline's nature, the least adaptive), followed by the mainstream and, unless the currently-held view that "there are no jobs in science" is shown to be false, followed by the young.

The absolute number of unemployed scientists is not yet high. But as scientists and mathematicians know well, it is often not the cumulative total but the rate and direction of the change that is significant.[5] Only 3 percent of previously trained physical scientists are currently unemployed, according to some sources (as compared to 13 percent of new Ph.D.s in mathematics), but that percentage has doubled in the past three years.[6] Even among fields enjoying a high demand, such as chemistry and environmental science, absolute unemployment increased in that same period. Thus, unemployment rose from 15,000 to 25,000, and there was a loss of 12,000 jobs in one year alone, in the U.S. chemical and allied products industry. Given the time lag in producing scientists (eight years on average from selecting the major to the Ph.D.), it is particularly hard to predict, no less adjust, supply and demand.

More doleful still is a comparison of unemployment between 1985 and 1993 of *new* Ph.D.s in the period immediately following graduation. The American Chemical Society's (ACS) annual survey of starting salaries

---

[4] See chap. 7 for an elaboration of this thesis.

[5] See numerous letters in *Chemical and Engineering News* on "Young Scientists' Network" (Nov. 2, 1992): p. 2; "Oversupply and Obsolescence" (Jan. 18, 1993): pp. 4-5; "What Future in Chemistry" (Jan. 18, 1993): p. 5; and "An Uncertain Career at Best" (Mar. 8, 1993): p. 3 for a sample.

[6] There are multiple sources for these figures, and slight differences, depending on who is counting and who is being counted. AIP reports in its latest graduate student handbook an unemployment rate for young physicists of 3.2%. *Science* reported in Sept. 1993 (vol. 261, p. 1765) an unemployment rate of 2.3% up from just over 1% in 1991 among "natural scientists," most likely including biologists. NAS finds physical and related scientists with a 2.1% unemployment rate ("Data Brief [draft 1] 1993 Employment Status of Doctoral Students and Engineers," NSF, Feb. 1995). Also see Peter D. Syverson, "Coping with Conflicting Data: The Employment Status of Recent Science and Engineering Ph.D.s," *CGS Communicator* 28, no. 7 (June 1995): pp. 8-9, 12.

Table I: Percentages of unemployment (white) and underemployment (shaded) of Ph.D.s in science and engineering by broad field (1993).

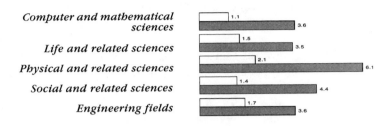

Computer and mathematical sciences	1.1 / 3.6
Life and related sciences	1.5 / 3.5
Physical and related sciences	2.1 / 6.1
Social and related sciences	1.4 / 4.4
Engineering fields	1.7 / 3.6

Source: NSF/SRS, 1993 Survey of Doctorate Recipients

shows that new Ph.D. unemployment climbed from 4.9% in 1985 to 11.4% in 1991 and 16.4% in 1993.[7] Even newly minted Ph.D.s (all fields of science) from prestigious institutions are graduating without offers— 13% of Princeton's Ph.D.s in 1993, as compared to 5% in 1992. Harder to measure is the *underemployment* of Ph.D.s in physical science. One indicator comes from the NSF's Science Resources Studies Division. Figures for 1993 (see Table I) show 6.1% of physical scientists to be underemployed. Another is that postdocs are having to stay on in their positions or take additional postdocs when they can't find career positions in academe or industry, causing the drought in postdoctoral positions for newer Ph.D.s (see chapter 4).[8]

The "Shortfall" and its Aftermath

In 1987 the National Science Foundation, then under the direction of Erich Bloch, undertook a study of the future supply of scientists and engineers. A shortfall was predicted based on the participation rate of 22-year-olds in natural science and the number of 22-year-olds in the population as a whole.[9] The study used the record high supply of science and engineering B.S. recipients (1983-84) *as a proxy for demand for all time.* Based on this unrealistic demand calculation, the study predicted a cumulative "shortfall" of between 675,000 and 692,000

---

[7] From the U.S. Department of Labor, quoted in *Manpower Comments* (Dec. 1993): p. 11.

[8] Betty M. Vetter, "Imbalance between Young Researchers and Employment Opportunities: A Working Paper," p. 18, Commission on Professionals in Science and Technology, Jul. 14, 1994.

[9] The study, begun in the Policy and Research Analysis Division in 1985, was never published but widely distributed and quoted. Its title was "Future Scarcities of Scientists and Engineers: Problems and Solutions," NSF working draft, Apr. 25, 1989.

science and engineering bachelors by 2006, followed by a proportion-
ate shortage of Ph.D.s.[10] By 1990, the notion that the science community had to beef up its supply was so widely accepted that Richard Atkinson,
incoming president of the American Association for the Advancement
of Science, called the supply issue for scientists and engineers a "national crisis in the making" in his inaugural address to the association
that year.[11]

In a remarkable reversal that took less than four years, the shortfall
all but evaporated, and a growing recognition that jobs, especially in
the physical sciences, were getting harder to find became cause for
concern. Colleges, universities, industrial employers, and even the national laboratories began to report staggering increases in the numbers of
Ph.D.s in physical science and mathematics *seeking* employment (200
on average for every academic job in physics and astronomy between
1990 and 1994, 1,000 during one year alone *per opening* in the mathematical sciences). Even the national press acknowledged an increasing
shortage of jobs.[12] A 1993 ACS employment survey called it "the worst
employment situation for chemists in the past 20 years," as a whopping
1,300 candidates registered at the ACS Employment Clearinghouse for
only 250 openings.[13]

The average newspaper reader was already aware that a growing
number of Ph.D.s in mathematics, engineering, and the physical sciences were being earned by citizens of other countries. Chemistry reported that of the 46 percent increase in chemistry Ph.D.s between 1980
and 1990, nearly all had gone to foreign nationals.[14] The shortfall advocates were not unaware of this influx, but most likely they saw it as
part of the evidence and the argument for the shortfall. Their thinking

---

[10] Alan Fechter, "Shortages and Shortfalls: Myths and Realities," presentation to the Convocation of Professional Engineering Societies and the National Association of Engineering, Jun. 1990 (available from the National Research Council). Published in *The Bridge* 20 (Fall 1990): pp. 16-20. For a discussion of the fallacy of the methodology, see also House Committee on Science, Space and Technology, Subcommittee on Investigations and Oversight, *Projecting Science and Engineering Personnel Requirements for the 1990s: How Good Are The Numbers? Hearing before the Committee on Science, Space, and Technology, Subcommittee on Investigations and Oversight,* 102nd Cong., 2nd sess., 8 Apr. 1992.

[11] Richard Atkinson, "Supply and Demand for Scientists and Engineers: A National Crisis in the Making," *Science* 248 (Apr. 27, 1990): pp. 425-432.

[12] For G. Pascal Zachary, writing in *The Wall Street Journal* as early as 1993, the situation was dismal, a "black hole" in scientist job rolls. (Apr. 14, 1993): pp. B1, B4. For physicist David Goodstein, it was a "rising tide of Ph.D.s that we seem helpless to stem." "Scientific Ph.D. Prob-lems," *The American Scholar* 62, vol. 2 (Spring 1993): p. 216. Peter T. Kilborn, writing in *The New York Times*, described the situation as "waves of unemployment" washing up on "science's shores." "Top Graduates in Science also put Dreams on Hold," (Jun. 6, 1993): pp. 1, 30.

[13] "Industry issues, jobs focus of ACS meeting," *Chemical and Engineering News* (Aug. 30, 1993): p. 9.

[14] "Complexities cloud long-term forecasts," *Chemical and Engineering News* (Oct. 19, 1992): p. 28.

must have gone something like this: with too few Americans (especially women and minority students) going into the sciences, mathematics, and engineering, foreign nationals were needed to fill the graduate student gap. But they would go home, or so it was thought. Even if they did stay here for the short-term, there was always the likelihood that they would leave if conditions in their homelands improved. So, throughout this period, the issue of foreign nationals was considered ancillary to the discussion of the shortfall.[15]

It was later confirmed in congressional hearings that the methodology used to project these shortages was, in the words of Representative Howard Wolpe, "flawed."[16] Indeed, those who constructed the shortfall argument did not consider a number of developments just then under way: the fact that large numbers of non-green-card-holding foreign scientists would find ways to change their immigration status and remain in the U.S. competing with citizens for jobs; and that with the breakup of the Soviet Union some of Russia's best and most promising scientists, engineers, and mathematicians would compete with American-trained scientists for jobs, and at bargain prices to boot.[17] President Bush's blanket invitation in 1992 to mainland Chinese students to stay in this country if they felt unsafe returning home after the 1989 violence of Tiananmen Square put an additional burden on the competition for jobs. (By far the majority of the foreign-born graduate students in science and engineering are mainland Chinese.)[18] In short, the impact of foreign nationals on the demand side of the equation at those early stages was not factored into the shortfall.

---

[15] For a range of views in the 1980s on foreign students in science, see the congressional Office of Technology Assessment's *Educating Scientists and Engineers; Grade School to Grad School* (Washington, D.C.: USGPO, 1988), p. 74; Donald R. Winkler, "The Costs and Benefits of Foreign Students in the U.S. Higher Education," *Journal of Public Policy* 4, no. 2 (1984): pp. 115-118; Elinor G. Barber, ed., *Foreign Student Flows*, Research Report no. 7 (New York: Institute for International Education, 1985); and NRC/OSEP, *Foreign and Foreign-Born Engineers in the United States: Infusing Talent, Raising Issues* (Washington, D.C.: National Academy Press, 1988).

[16] House Committee on Science, Space and Technology, *Projecting Science and Engineering Personnel Requirements for the 1990s: How Good Are the Numbers? Hearing before the Subcommittee on Investigations and Oversight of the Committee on Science, Space and Technology.* 102nd Cong., 2nd sess., 8 Apr. 1992, p. 2.

[17] Stephen Rosen, founder and chairman of a new nonprofit agency, the New York-based Science and Technology Advisory Board, estimates that more than 4,000 scientists emigrated from the Soviet Union to the U.S. in 1990-1992. See, "For Emigres: 12 Steps to Capitalism," *The New York Times* (May 21, 1992): p. B1. Of these, there are about 50 Russian scientists currently holding professorships in U.S. universities and another 25 from other former Soviet states; another 200 have found research positions in industrial and laboratory jobs. Even though the flood is tapering off, the perception is that universities are able to recruit three Russian scientists for the price of two Americans—and that they do.

[18] President Bush's response to Tiananmen Square in 1989 was to issue the Chinese Student Protection Act (actually an executive order) in Nov. 1992 which permitted Chinese graduate students then on temporary visas in the U.S. to apply for permanent visa status.

Since we cannot know how many of the 100,000 foreign graduate students studying in the U.S. at any one time will stay, it is difficult to make more than short-term estimates as to what the impact of foreign nationals on demand will be. We have only indicators, such as the annual National Research Council *Survey of Doctorate Recipients*, which found that the percentage of noncitizens on temporary visas with plans to remain and who had definite commitments after graduate school rose from 23% in 1972 to 58% in 1992.[19] If these foreign scholars did find jobs, then the proportion of foreign-born scientists in the nation's doctoral work force (already 13.6% in 1989) has increased still more. With foreign nationals winning between 45 and 60% of the U.S. Ph.D.s granted in math, computer science, the physical sciences, and engineering, their proportion of the work force, if the 58% staying rate of 1992 holds, must continue to climb.[20] In hindsight, a policy analyst is tempted to conclude that, however flawed the methodology used to predict it, there may have been a connection between the widely ballyhooed shortfall and the present job crunch. A real decline in the 1980s of U.S.-born applicants for graduate study in math, science, and engineering caused academic departments eager to fill their graduate slots to solicit and respond more positively to applications from abroad, assuming that foreign students would end up back home.

That the shortfall died hard is evidenced by its brief reappearance as part of the Immigration Act of 1990. This bill contained provisions that allowed employers to recruit outside the United States without going through the usual certification that they could not find qualified Americans. The Department of Labor (DOL) was required by the act to initiate a pilot program to identify up to ten fields in which there were labor shortages. By March 1993, on assignment from DOL, a University of Michigan researcher identified shortages in six technical specialties distributed over twenty-one states. When the Young Scientists' Network and others saw biological sciences, chemistry, computer science, and three areas of engineering on those lists, they undertook a letter-writing campaign joined by members of the professional scientific and engineering societies. The selective preferences section of the act was repealed only in 1994 after the annual number of job-based visas nearly

---

[19] Betty Vetter estimated that about 20% leave the U.S. immediately upon receipt of the degree, but about half remain to compete for jobs in the U.S. See her report in *Manpower Comments* 31, no. 2 (Mar. 1994): p. 3. NSF estimates that from 54 to 68% of foreign-born Ph.D.s are electing to pursue careers in the U.S., about equally distributed between academe and industry. See *Science* 261 (24 Sept. 1993): p. 1769.

[20] "Foreign Nationals Change the Face of Science," *Science* 261 (24 Sept. 1993): pp. 1769-1770. By field some of those proportions are already higher: 22% of doctoral chemists working in pharmaceuticals are categorized as naturalized citizens, permanent residents, or are on temporary visas.

tripled from 54,000 to 140,000. About one third of the visa holders were scientists.[21]

One can ask whether it is ever reasonable to talk about supply, quantitatively or prescriptively, without more than back-of-the-envelope estimates of demand, and whether the federal government and the professional societies ever really know (or know soon enough) what's going on in the science labor market. We seem to count on a variation of Adam Smith's "invisible hand" to create a productive equilibrium from all the thousands of individual fee-for-labor transactions that constitute science employment. Short of adding full-fledged human resources planning to the national science agencies' responsibilities, are there ways of coordinating the training and employment of scientists so as to protect our human capital in science, engineering, and mathematics from the vicissitudes of cyclical and structural downturns?

We will return to supply and demand issues in chapters 5, 6, and 7, but here it is perhaps appropriate to foreshadow our answer to these questions: Government is a necessary partner in protecting our human resources from underachievement and underemployment, but it cannot do the job alone. Scientists, individually and through professional organizations, must start paying close attention to human resources issues—and not just when there is a shortage or a sudden oversupply. *Our* question must become *their* question: What can be done to coordinate the nation's obvious need for science with a sustainable demand for scientists? One place to begin is by collecting better, more meaningful data.[22]

Data Collection and Interpretation

Not surprisingly, the debate over the shortfall raised important questions about data collection in the government's (and others') monitoring of supply and demand for research scientists. In late spring 1994, the Alfred P. Sloan Foundation invited a group of professionals familiar with human resources data bases to explore the "Imbalance between Young Researchers and Employment Opportunities" at a one-day meeting in Washington, D.C. Sloan had already funded the late Betty Vetter, founder and director of the Commission on Professionals in Science and Technology, to catalog existing data sources and analyze their strengths and weaknesses.[23] Since any inventory of existing data bases

---

[21] Boyce Rensberger, "Scientific Ranks Outpace Funds," *Washington Post* (Dec. 25, 1994): pp. A1, A20.

[22] See especially Betty M. Vetter, "Setting the Record Straight: Shortages in Perspective," Occasional Paper 92-4, Commission on Professionals in Science and Technology, Washington, D. C., Jan. 1993.

[23] Betty M. Vetter, "Imbalance between."

is rare, and an examination of their strengths and weaknesses rarer still, our analysis builds on Vetter's rich description of the traditional sources of information about human resources in science.

To the observer, the most obvious defect in the government's data-collecting activity is that it focuses almost exclusively on supply, and doesn't attempt to track employers' behavior, turnover rates, or other indicators as to how well supply and demand are in balance. The sources of supply data are impressive (see below) but information is slow in coming, sometimes because of cost-cutting which postpones analysis until long after data have been collected, sometimes because of changes in scope or methodology, making data sets difficult to compare. For employer surveys, one has to look to the professional societies.[24] What is missing from the government's data-collection function are: (1) employer surveys by industry and sector providing a frequently updated systematic review of where jobs in science currently are or likely to be; and (2), a quick-response unit within the NSF or NAS that can provide selective short-term reviews of the supply and demand picture as often as every six months.

One objection to any demand analysis is that it is hard to do.[25] It is much easier to track supply since the agency has only to survey academic departments to find out how many scientists are in the pipeline and how many will graduate this year and next. Another reason demand analysis gets short shrift is that the government believes it can do something about supply, such as cut back or augment graduate stipends, while it is not at all obvious how public policy could affect demand (see chapter 7 for a counterview). Still, even partial demand analyses would be better than none: for example, a survey of college and university department chairs to measure the impact on new hires of the lifting of mandatory retirement dates. If it can be ascertained that 10 percent of senior faculty in the physical sciences are postponing retirement by one, two, or five years, the percentage change in the availability of academic openings can be calculated.

Because supply data are favored, there are many sources of information about the supply of scientists but, given the size of the survey populations and the cost of analyzing them, the data are often not current. For example, throughout 1993-94, policy analysts had to work

---

[24] The American Institute of Physics tracks employment on the demand side, as does the Engineering Workforce Commission, a privately funded arm of the American Association of Engineering Societies—but only for engineers. Betty Vetter's own Commission on Professionals in Science and Technology tried, but with limited funds, to study demand.

[25] Though it would be easy for the federal government, which employs 7.5% of all the scientists and engineers in the U.S., to calculate its own employment demand. It would be at least a beginning and much would be learned about doing demand surveys.

with 1989 data, knowing that the situation had radically changed; and only in late 1994 did 1991 data become available. Anecdotal information, on the other hand, while fresh, wide-ranging, and more nuanced than responses to survey questionnaires, tends not to be representative and therefore not reliable. But in either case, those who construct the survey questions, according to Vetter, do not always have in mind the kinds of information public policy users need.[26]

Of the large multiple field data bases, the annual census or *Survey of Earned Doctorates* (SED) is the only coverage of everyone in a particular category—in this instance, the doctoral degrees awarded each year to citizens and noncitizens.[27] Not limited to science and engineering, the SED is supported by five federal agencies.[28] It includes age, sex, race, ethnicity, and citizenship of the recipients; their principal source of support through graduate school; their plans for further study or employment at the time of graduation; and whether they still seek or have already located a postdoctoral position.[29] The SED is very useful in providing—by means of an analysis of postgraduation plans of selected Ph.D. classes from 1982 through 1992—two indicators of changes in job prospects: changes in the percentages of scientists having job commitments at the time of graduation, and changes in the percentages of new Ph.D.s willing to pursue postdoctoral positions. This latter figure increased from 39% to 46% over the decade, most likely linked to the higher percentage of graduates who did not get jobs the previous year.[30]

While these data give early indications of trends in available employment, they are but "snapshots" of a single moment in time. Also needed for every class of doctoral students, we would argue, are data on how long it took them to locate employment (either permanent or postdoctoral positions) and whether they identify themselves as still in the field of their Ph.D. training. Such information can only be derived indirectly from other data gathered by the National Academy of Science's (NAS) National Research Council and published by NSF.

The *Survey of Doctorate Recipients* (SDR) is a large biennial *sampling* (not a census) of doctorates earned in the United States. Unfor-

---

[26] Betty Vetter, "Imbalance between."

[27] All academic disciplines are included, but it is relatively simple to disaggregate by discipline or by families of disciplines.

[28] NSF, NIH, National Endowment for the Humanities, and the Departments of Education and Agriculture. The survey is also known as the Doctorate Records File (DRF).

[29] Other information is solicited but these categories bear most directly on the employment issue.

[30] Among these recent doctorates as a group, 4% were still postdoctoral students five and six years after earning the doctorate (1991 data). See Vetter, "Imbalance between," p. 8.

tunately, the sample has recently been reduced by half to cut costs and is now restricted to doctorate-holders currently employed in the U.S., which makes comparisons with earlier years difficult.[31] But even without these limitations, the survey takes so long to collect and analyze that users must be satisfied with two- and sometimes four-year-old information. There is important information in the SDR, but it is too slow in coming to be useful in picking out trends.

Information about postdoctorals is embedded in the National Science Foundation's *Survey of Graduate Science and Engineering Student Support and Postdoctorates,* and in other NAS occasional studies of specific fields. Among these are two old but important studies of postdoctorals in science and engineering, *Non-Faculty Doctoral Research Staff in Science and Engineering in U.S. Universities,* published in 1978, and a 1981 study, *Postdoctoral Appointments and Disappointments.* NAS also published a series of studies from the mid-1970s to 1984 entitled *Academic Science: Scientists and Engineers.*

In addition to multiple-field studies, there are single-discipline data bases, including surveys of their members by the American Institute of Physics (AIP), the American Chemical Society, the American Geological Institute (AGI), and others. While these surveys provide more up-to-date information than federal sources, they focus on single fields, ask different questions, and very often use incompatible time-frames.[32] Still, when researchers are willing to do the tedious follow-ups that are often required, the findings can be illuminating.[33]

It is our contention that supply data alone are an insufficient base for developing public policy. The other side of the equation, demand, helps locate the opportunities potentially hit or missed. An organization with stable funding needs to do this on an ongoing basis, else future crosscutting analyses will suffer from the same woes detailed above. In other words, we have inherited a data problem—one every-

---

[31] The SDR is sponsored by the NSF, National Endowment for the Humanities, NIH, and the Department of Energy and has been conducted since 1973. It was known until 1977 as the *Survey of Doctoral Scientists and Engineers.* In each year, new Ph.D. recipients from the previous two years are added to the sampling frame, and the two earliest years of doctorates are deleted to retain a 42-year cohort span. In 1991, the age range was extended to those age 75 or younger, and while the initial sample was reduced by about half, the response rates were increased by telephone follow-up. For this reason, and because the survey hit the field much later than in the past, the 1991 data cannot be compared with that of earlier surveys.

[32] Betty M. Vetter, "Imbalance between."

[33] An AIP physics survey undertaken in 1992 yielded a 52% response. After follow-up phoning to the recipients' doctoral granting institutions, the yield was 78%—very impressive for a survey. See Kate Kirby and Roman Czujko, "The Physics Job Market: Bleak for Young Physicists," *Physics Today* (Dec. 1993): pp. 22-27; Susanne D. Ellis, "Initial Employment of Physics Doctorate Recipients: Class of 1992," *Physics Today,* same issue, pp. 29-33.

body acknowledges. The best response to date has been the monitoring work of the Commission on Professionals in Science and Technology, a nonprofit, nongovernmental organization. With only modest staff and funding, the commission has so far only been able to provide diagnostics on a short-term basis. Clearly, there is important empirical work still to be done. The science community needs to be mobilized either to fund a repository of supply *and* demand information, or to convene a group to determine the scope of the task and the investment needed to provide reliable information for all. If done well, there are many potential users: students, suppliers, employers, and analysts.

Supply and Demand Imbalances: Cyclic or Structural?

Many can now point to the reasons for the lack of a shortfall, but it is not at all clear whether the shifts in employment are cyclical, or longer-term and structural and therefore resistant to palliatives. The fact that there was a similar (though not entirely comparable) shortage of jobs for trained physical scientists in the early 1970s fuels the cyclic argument. Indeed, as early as 1965, economist Allan Cartter, then vice president of the American Council on Education (ACE), calculated that there would be a 33 percent oversupply of scientists for university employment by the 1970s and as much as a 50 percent surplus in the 1980s.[34] He was right about university employment in the 1970s, but wrong about the 1980s. How come? Alan Fechter offers one answer: "Industry was a strong source of demand for Ph.D.s in the period after 1975; Cartter was only talking about faculty positions."[35] Another reason is that many state universities were building new Ph.D. programs in that same period and needed research-trained faculty. The new university research programs were important sources of jobs, but were they the best place to do science?

Sociologist of science David Drew thinks not. Drawing on extensive field-study interviews and large data sets from ACE and the Higher Education Research Institute (HERI), Drew found in the late 1970s and 1980s (not a period of decline) that a "forgotten army of highly capable academic scientists [were] rusting away their skills in the nation's peripheral universities."[36] Because these institutions could not adequately support their professors' research, large numbers of young scientists were not doing the science of which they were capable (measured in grants won and papers published). When Drew correlated a whole host

---

[34] Allan M. Cartter, *An Assessment of Quality in Graduate Education* (Washington, D. C.: ACE, 1965), p. 270, quoted in David E. Drew, *Strengthening Academic Science* (New York: Prager, 1985), p. 17.

[35] Alan Fechter, personal communication to the authors.

[36] Drew, introduction to *Strengthening Academic Science*.

of factors with such measures of productivity, he found that the prestige of a Ph.D.'s alma mater and the resources of the employing institution accounted for significant variation across all fields.[37] The prestige factor, he explained in his 1985 book, *Strengthening Academic Science*, leads to an "accumulated advantage," and lack of prestige to an "accumulated disadvantage." A prestige-driven system of grants-making contributes to a structural problem, he concluded, placing both scientific talent and future potential at risk.[38]

A case could be made (see chapter 2) that the current situation is neither cyclical nor structural, but a rare coincidence of factors that might never come together again. We, however, subscribe to the structural view: the sky may not be falling, but prospects for careers in science are receding under thickening clouds. What were once transitory discontinuities have become chronic imbalances between the supply of, and demand for, science professionals. Recovery will not be fueled by dollars alone, and may be so gradual that it goes unnoticed. Structural change is required, and planning, or at least the kind of analysis that leads to planning, is desperately needed. Cyclical problems tend to go away. People who survive forget; people who do not survive are never heard from again. Structural problems are both more intransigent and more promising. If what is broken can really be fixed, then it need never be "broken" again.

We may not be able to determine with certainty to what extent the current job crunch is structural, but we can certainly pay greater attention to three factors: first, the operation of an imperfect market economy for scientists (made less perfect by shifting corporate attitudes); second, the failure of a large portion (but by no means all) of the science professoriate to prepare their students for a wider variety of careers; and third, a public policy that, ever since Vannevar Bush, has assumed that the availability of a well-trained scientific elite, together with government funding of some areas of scientific research, would continue in perpetuity to fuel demand.

Conclusion

The federal government has been a key player in structuring human resources policy for science. Ever since passage of Public Law 85-86, the National Defense Education Act of 1958, the government has supported the training of pre- and postdoctoral students. The part played

---

[37] Ibid., p. 115.

[38] The "accumulated advantage" hypothesis was first observed by sociologist Robert Merton, later elaborated by Stephen and Jonathan Cole. For an update, see Robert K. Merton, "The Matthew Effect in Science, II," *Isis* 79 (1988): pp. 606-623.

by NSF, NASA, NIH, DOE (Energy), DOD, and USDA (Agriculture) in sustaining and expanding the pool of scientific talent is an impressive legacy of programmatic intervention. Federal agencies continue today to influence career choice, but on what basis do they set their human resources priorities, or even the *nature* of their support? On the one hand, there is research support, directed to senior and well-established principal investigators, favoring the best-equipped research universities, and designed to support graduate assistants and postdoctoral professionals. On the other hand, there are graduate fellowships targeted for individuals showing high promise (and, in the case of NSF and NIH, for underrepresented minority groups as well), which can be taken to an institution of choice. On occasion the federal government has also provided direct support so that certain institutions can become either "centers of excellence" or magnets for research in certain areas.

But the bulk of federal funding in the past has been research-driven; that is, in support of an investigative program with graduate training and postgraduate employment as ancillary benefits. Science graduates find themselves actively recruited during their training period but on their own once degrees and postdocs are behind them. Much as their students, mentors are helpless in the face of diminishing demand. Indeed, many do not know (or do not bother to find out) what opportunities for students exist outside of academic or federally-funded research institutions. The professional societies provide good how-to publications for graduates, but these are not (yet) required reading for their professors.

The result is an odd and inefficient combination of a planned and market-driven economy in science—planned in the sense that without government research support there would be few opportunities for training, unplanned in that there are no bridges established by government or industry to span the gap between supply and demand. For the lucky few who land jobs appropriate to their training, the system works well. For the others, science ceases to be a viable career option just when they are ready to make a contribution.

2

What is a Scientist?
And What Does a Scientist Do?

PERSISTENCE OF PERCEPTIONS FROM A BYGONE ERA

T HE PROSPECTS for a career in science have changed dramatically in one generation. This is true despite the fact that the nation's *need* for science is no less than it was in 1945. As we have noted, Vannevar Bush wanted the funding of basic research intertwined with training; hence his preference for universities over industrial or national labs. Indeed, in his many essays and talks on the subject, he described college and university scientists as "teachers and investigators," in that order, and his proposal for the establishment of a "national research foundation" (later the National Science Foundation) included funding for 24,000 undergraduate and 900 graduate fellowships to be awarded annually.[1]

Bush favored universities for many reasons: he didn't trust industry's commitment to basic research and he was grateful that there had been an academic reserve in science that the U.S. could draw on during the war. But the overwhelming justification for a national research foundation to sustain university scientists was that the same funding would support teaching and research. University-based research would uniquely encourage and engage the next generation of scientists as no other institutional arrangement could. Driving Vannevar Bush's *Science the Endless Frontier* was a "social compact." On the one hand, judgment of scientific merit would be delegated to expert peers in return for progress that, in the long run, would benefit the nation in terms of its military security, economic productivity, and enhanced quality of life. On the

---

[1] Vannevar Bush, *Science the Endless Frontier: A Report to the President* (Washington, D.C.: USGPO, 1945) reprinted by the NSF, 1960; see also Vannevar Bush, *Endless Horizons* (Washington, D.C.: Public Affairs Press, 1946), p. 69.

other hand, scientists would benefit from federal funding and public support, both for their production of new knowledge and for successive cohorts of trained personnel.[2] These were the conditions of continuity between generations, of the "best and brightest" selecting their offspring and launching them on careers that would (it was assumed) emulate their own.

There was just one flaw in the plan: implicit was the premise that an ever-growing supply of scientists would stimulate new demand for scientific expertise, not just in government and universities, but in industry and other professional venues. Vannevar Bush never expected that, owing in large measure to federal funding, university scientists would in the next forty years produce not just the national science reserve he envisioned, but a growing number of young Ph.D.s many of whom wanted nothing more (and nothing less) than to be university scientists themselves. The absence of a plan to complement supply with demand is one source of the inherent structural problem in American science today: not enough versatility in training. Another is insufficient industrial demand to create sustained employment, even for those willing to forgo the status and autonomy of the professoriate.

The NSF went into operation in 1950 with an annual budget of $3.5 million, a figure that grew over the next forty years to just over $3.3 *billion* (1994 figures), an increase of about 1,000 times.[3] And, as Vannevar Bush had hoped, the nation's primary science agency acted to spur research spending elsewhere in the federal government and in industry. By 1993, of total federal R&D of $73 billion (60 percent defense-related), more than $15 billion (largely nondefense) was flowing in research and development monies to the nation's universities. It was increasingly obvious that the economy and national security were singularly dependent both on new developments in science and technology and on maintaining the science-technology labor force. Not surprisingly, in a period when research outlays were doubling and doubling again, able young people were attracted to research science. Although it is part of the "mystique" of science that practitioners value the intrinsic challenge more than extrinsic rewards, the fact that science was seen as a pathway to secure and lucrative employment, not to mention status and the nation's good will, made recruitment easy—even during recessionary cycles.

With the end of the cold war, however, competition for federal dollars and a shift in national priorities toward improving industrial competitiveness changed the career calculus. While the NSF budget saw

---

[2] See Daryl E. Chubin, "How Large an R&D Enterprise?" in *The Fragile Contract*, eds. D. Guston and K. Keniston (Cambridge, Mass.: MIT Press, 1994), pp. 118-144.

[3] The foundation was established by Public Law 81-507, signed May 10, 1950 by President Truman.

manifold increases, the number of applicants for funding and the cost of each research proposal increased as well, with federal support available (in 1992) for only one acceptable research proposal out of every five.[4] As our inquiries attest (see especially chapter 4), a career in science in the twenty-first century appears uncertain, both in terms of the expected demand for professionals and the kinds of opportunities by sector and institution. Young scientists now have to think about financial security, career advancement, and career satisfaction, often in *that* order, not in terms of the idealized notions of yesteryear.

The Idealized View: Examples and Counterexamples

The sociological literature on careers in science exhibits a preoccupation with physical scientists in university settings who favor the tasks of research, which garners the rewards of an adoring community. Their careers ring with accomplishment and are idealized through books such as sociologist Harriet Zuckerman's 1977 *Scientific Elites: Nobel Laureates in the United States*.[5] What is notable about this literature is its glorification of a single career path involving research as craftwork.[6] Zuckerman goes so far as to suggest that because half of all Nobel laureates were themselves trained by Nobelists, there is something mystical about the mentor-student relationship. This fascination with academic luminaries, their accolades, and their legacy of students may have seemed fitting a generation ago when the opportunities for university careers were abundant. Such a fascination now appears misplaced and distracting. But even then the idealized view was overdrawn.[7]

Support of American science used to be more diversified than it is today, and American scientists seemed more willing—or so it appears in retrospect—to assume responsibility for their research support. Evidence for this can be found in the establishment of such philanthropic institutions as Research Corporation, a kind of cooperative to license faculty-generated patents, the royalties from which would flow back

---

[4] Across all agencies funding for R&D doubled between 1980 and 1992, but competitors quadrupled. Government-University-Industry Research Roundtable, *Fateful Choices: The Future of the U.S. Academic Research Enterprise* (Washington, D.C.: National Academy Press, 1992).

[5] Harriet Zuckerman, *Scientific Elites: Nobel Laureates in the United States* (New York: Free Press, 1977).

[6] Other representative works from historians and philosophers as well as sociologists include: Jerome Ravetz, *Scientific Knowledge and Its Social Problems* (Oxford, U.K.: Oxford University Press, 1971); Thomas S. Kuhn, "The Essential Tension: Tradition and Innovation in Scientific Research," a chapter in *The Essential Tension: Selected Studies in Scientific Tradition and Change* (Chicago: University of Chicago Press, 1977), pp. 225-239; and Jonathan R. Cole and Stephen Cole, *Social Stratification in Science* (Chicago: University of Chicago Press, 1973).

[7] Alan L. Porter et al., "The Doctoral Dissertation: Its Role in Research and Non-Research Careers," *American Scientist* 70 (1982): pp. 475-481.

into scholarly science. Research Corporation, founded in 1912, also inspired a host of university-linked foundations that aimed to use the results of research to support further investigations. Over the years, Research Corporation has evaluated roughly 14,000 inventions and granted in excess of $150 million for projects independently proposed by faculty scientists.[8]

In 1925 the University of Wisconsin established its Wisconsin Alumni Research Foundation to "promote, encourage and aid science investment and research at that university."[9] How was this to be done? By "providing means and machinery for the development and patenting of faculty discoveries." By 1931, royalties on foundation patents generated an income of $1,000 per day, and a reserve endowment had grown to $500,000, producing more income for faculty research. (In 1994 gross earnings from patent royalties topped $15.8 million.) The University of Cincinnati in that same period was operating its basic science research lab on funds derived from patents given as dividends on its stock in a holding company. MIT had a policy of claiming rights to patentable discoveries made by faculty members.

Also of note is the role played in the first four decades of the twentieth century by the nation's scientific and professional organizations on behalf of their members and, as they saw it, on behalf of American science and society. Issues of science policy were not just acknowledged but debated by the American Association for the Advancement of Science. Absent the big government the nation has grown used to since WWII, the earlier period was characterized by grass-roots collaboration between self-governing bodies.

Take, for example, the thorny issue of whether or not "scientific property"—theories or discoveries of laws—could (legally) or should (morally) be patentable. As industry began to rely more on basic research, scientists and professional societies expressed concern about how to protect discoveries which did not fall under the U.S. patent code, and whether the faculty inventor or his university should own the patents.[10] Europeans were sufficiently interested in the matter of scientific property after World War I to pressure the League of Nations

---

[8] For an account of the philanthropic motives of Research Corporation's founder, see p. 147 and Frank Cameron, *Cottrell: Samaritan of Science* (Garden City, N.Y.: Country Life Press, 1952; reprint, Tucson, Ariz.: Research Corporation, 1993).

[9] This language and the details that follow are taken from a 1934 occasional paper published by the American Association for the Advancement of Science, "The Protection by Patents of Scientific Discoveries" (New York: The Science Press, 1934). The publication originated as a report of the AAAS Committee on Patents, Copyrights, and Trade Marks, of which Joseph Rossman was chair, and F. G. Cottrell, W. A. Hull, and A. E. Woods members.

[10] U.S. patents are issued only to the inventor but the rights can be assigned to a university or other employer.

to explore possible positions, but until 1930 there was little U.S. interest in patent ownership issues involving scientific discoveries and their end uses. Once that interest was expressed, however, a dialogue began that involved the American Bar Association, the American Association for the Advancement of Science, and the Association of American Colleges.[11] In the modern world such efforts would probably be initiated by the National Academy of Sciences, or federal agencies such as the National Science Foundation, leaving the professional associations to respond to official policy papers.

The debate over scientific property and the foundations that were established to transfer invention-generated royalties back to science represent a high-water mark in the history of American science in relation to technology. It also anticipates the "added value" argument we will raise in chapter 7. For if, in fact, basic research adds value to the economy, then American scientists—the ordinary as well as the extraordinary—should be well supported. But our images of American scientists today are not of ordinary men and women. Rather, they are drawn from the adventures of pioneering geniuses and headstrong researchers such as Hans Bethe, James Watson, Barbara McClintock, Linus Pauling, and Richard Feynman. For the student who aborts a career in graduate school or who doesn't succeed thereafter (where success is defined as following in the mentor's footsteps), failure is personal, the perceived effect of emotional or intellectual unfitness. Indeed, respondents to our survey of applicants for college and university jobs (see chapter 4) exhibited these feelings all too often.[12]

Is there another venue for career training and planning besides mentorship?[13] And can there be support for scientists that leaves them less dependent on their sponsors and on the vicissitudes of institutional budgets? How we act on these issues may determine whether science will remain a viable career option in the future.

More or Less of the Same?

The employment quandary of the 1990s has been addressed relentlessly by the U.S. physics community, and in recent months by the American Chemical Society as well. One view, represented by physi-

---

[11] The final positions taken were: affirmative on the right of university research scientists to patent their work and inclined to recommend that they not profit personally, but transfer patents to quasi-public bodies; and negative on the desirability of patenting scientific theory and discovery.

[12] See also Roger G. Krohn, *The Social Shaping of Science: Institutions, Ideology, and Careers in Science* (Westport, Conn.: Greenwood Publishing, 1971).

[13] In Europe one's rank on a series of examinations *(Concours)* determines eligibility for fellowships, postdocs, and faculty or other professional research positions.

cist and former AAAS president Leon Lederman, in *Science: The End of a Frontier* (a twist on Bush's title), is what we are tempted to call "more of the same":[14] if American science is to preserve its scope and achievement, federal expenditures for research must be increased. This view betrays a single—and narrow—mindedness about the preferred career path for scientists, in which young physicists, like their forebears, are to ply the traditional academic investigator route. Lederman's 1990 survey of researchers at fifty major universities, undertaken for the AAAS, did contribute to a realistic assessment of the prospects for initiating or sustaining a research career.[15] His solution is more of the same because it calls for more federal funding rather than a change in the way we support science and scientific careers.

More dramatic is the proposal from the physics community (and from some in chemistry as well) that in order to survive, the scientific community should reduce the supply of research scientists. John M. Rowell, a condensed-matter physicist, suggests two ways of "shrinking the field" to match supply with demand. "The first is painful: allow funding difficulties to continue, which will cause people to give up research in frustration. The second is to voluntarily shrink the field. This is accomplished by every professor taking fewer students, by the universities not filling all the faculty positions that become available, by the national labs not maintaining their size simply for historic reasons, and by industry being honest about its future need for scientists."[16] Other scientists, among them David Goodstein, physicist and vice provost at Caltech, concede that the exponential growth of American science since the end of WWII had to come to an end. And to the extent that expansion of university science departments was predicated on that growth rate, they have become dysfunctional. There won't be, there can't be, a research professorship for every aspiring Ph.D. in physics.[17] We agree but, since that never was the intention of the 1945 social compact Vannevar Bush envisioned, why should the solution be a cut-

---

[14] Sheila Tobias calls it that in "The Jobs Situation: Must it be More and Less of the Same?" *APS News* (Apr. 1994): p. 8.

[15] Leon M. Lederman, *Science: The End of the Frontier* (Washington, D.C.: AAAS, 1991). At about the same time as Lederman's 1990 report, APS surveyed young physics faculty (that is, those with traditional jobs in physics) at all 177 Ph.D.-granting universities in the U.S. The responses revealed a decline in success rates of proposals submitted for federal research funding, compared to a similar survey conducted in 1977. See Roman Czujko, et al., *Their Most Productive Years, Report on the 1990 Survey of Young Physics Faculty* (Washington, D.C.: APS, 1991).

[16] John M. Rowell, "Condensed Matter Physics in a Market Economy," *Physics Today* (Mar. 1992): p. 47.

[17] David Goodstein, "Scientific Elites and Scientific Illiterates," in *Engineering and Science*, Caltech Alumni Magazine (Spring 1993): pp. 15-19; also published with the same title in *Ethics, Values, and the Promise of Science*, Sigma Xi Forum Proceedings (Research Triangle, N.C.: Sigma Xi, 1993), pp. 61-76.

back on Ph.D. production? Why not train physicists (and chemists and geologists and astronomers) to do more diverse kinds of work?

A variant on the Goodstein call for long-term academic birth control is that of physicist Hellmut Fritzsche of the University of Chicago and others who believe that the problem is not exactly cyclical but not structural either. Rather, we are experiencing a *coincidence of events* that have compounded one another: the admission of 20,000 Chinese scientists in a ten-year period, the sudden and unexpected availability of Russian scientists, three years of downsizing and even elimination of many industrial labs, changes in mandatory retirement age for faculty, and the end of the cold war. Given the vitality of American science, believes Fritzsche, there is no need to make fundamental alterations either in the supply or demand sides of the human resources equation, only to do some production control (elimination of third-tier Ph.D. programs) over the short run.[18]

Based on analyses by the American Institute of Physics' Employment Statistics Division, Richard Werthamer, former executive secretary of American Physical Society, appears to support our contention that the role of researcher ought not be the only path to professional fulfillment.[19] This mentality, he says, belongs to an earlier era. The challenge now is to demonstrate

> . . . how science as a way of knowing is a sound foundation for a multifaceted career; a sequence of opportunities that exploit the skills of the scientist for the national good while, at the same time, rewarding creativity, autonomy, problem-solving, industriousness, and the yearning for knowledge.[20]

In response to this kind of argument and pressure from younger scientists, the APS approved a remarkable directive in April 1994:

> . . . it is important for faculty members to make all their undergraduate and graduate students aware of the realities of the job market and to encourage them to prepare for a broad range of careers. Academic physics departments are urged to reexamine their programs in light of the changing opportunities.[21]

The blandness of this statement belies its revolutionary character. It calls for nothing less than a change in the culture of graduate training.

---

[18] Hellmut Fritzsche, personal communication to the authors.

[19] N. Richard Werthamer, "The Employment Problem—Cyclical or Structural?" *APS Issues* 2 (Mar. 1993): pp. 17-18.

[20] Ibid.

[21] Reported in *APS News*, Apr. 1994.

Academic departments, however, are going to need direction and tangible support if such a transformation of mission is to be accomplished.

Although chemistry, in contrast to physics, places more Ph.D. recipients in industry than in academia, the decline in industrial basic research has increased chemists' vulnerability to employment downturns as well.[22] In a recent presentation, Martha Krebs, director of research for the Department of Energy, presented evidence of a substantial five-year decline in industrial spending on R&D. Indeed, as this book was in preparation, spokespersons for research at Dupont and other companies announced that they would not be hiring as many new Ph.D. chemists in the immediate future.[23] Unemployment has spurred the American Chemical Society to track its members' careers more thoroughly, particularly those holding temporary positions. ACS has formally acknowledged the need to change both the perceptions and realities of science as a career. In addition to increased government funding for research, participants in an ACS interactive colloquium in April 1994 called for more direct fellowships to students, and a broader exposure to industrial chemistry in graduate school even at the expense of thesis research time.[24] Other suggestions were incorporation of a "minor" field in graduate school, and student attendance at courses and seminars outside immediate specialties.

In addition to APS' and ACS' reassessments, leading scientists are beginning to call for less specialization in graduate and even undergraduate training (see chapters 5 and 6). Marvin Goldberger, former president of Caltech, wants "training for versatility" begun on the undergraduate level in physics, with courses on applications substituting for part of the standard curriculum. To demonstrate, he has prepared fifty modules that teach advanced theory through applications. John Armstrong, former vice president for research at IBM, would have graduate students in science spend summers away from the academy in order to understand better how science fits into a variety of industrial situations. Brian Schwartz, professor of physics at Brooklyn College, now requires Ph.D. physics students to study C and C++ (computer

---

[22] The American Chemical Society doesn't have an exact breakdown of chemistry Ph.D.s by sectors: industry, national labs, and academe. But of the total 200,000 chemists employed, approximately 150,000 are members of the ACS. Those members' employment characteristics are as follows: 61% industry and government labs, 39% academic or on research contract. Personal communication from Ned D. Heindel, ACS president.

[23] In "New Realities of Industrial Employment: A Panel Discussion," *Preparing for the 21st Century: Human Resources in Science and Technology* (Washington, D.C.: Commission on Professionals in Science and Technology, 1992).

[24] *Shaping the Future: The Chemical Research Environment in the Next Century, A Presidential Interactive Colloquium* (Washington D.C.: American Chemical Society, 1994).

programming languages used in industry and not conventionally part of the curriculum) and other technical skills before letting them loose on the job market. And Mark McDermott, past physics chair at the University of Washington, is doing what APS calls for: having his faculty reexamine their programs in light of the new reality. He puts it bluntly when he tells his colleagues, "Instead of training them to do what we do, we should be assisting our students to learn what they need to learn." The most constructive way to find out what future scientists may need to learn, says Robert Sproull, former president of University of Rochester, is to expose faculty who are training the next generation of scientists to the world outside the university.[25]

Toward a New Social Compact

Vannevar Bush had a clear sense of the social responsibility of science in the immediate postwar period. He wanted to see a certain ratio maintained between basic and applied research. What he didn't foresee is that—thanks to federal support, a forty-year record of remarkable achievements, and the appeal of the university lifestyle—university-based science would come to dominate American science and disparage all but the discovery of new knowledge, including teaching itself. David Goodstein anticipates that whatever we do, "the future of American science will be very different from the past."[26] But in what ways? Will it be more or less of the same, or different in character? And what will be the impact of impending changes on science as a career? Are the young to be trained in the image of their forebears only to be buffeted by forces they are unprepared for? Or, are they to take the lead in forging new combinations of tasks that will make them more valuable to society?[27]

The needs of the society in which scientists work and which largely sustains them cannot be overlooked. Congressman George Brown, former chairman of the House Committee on Science, Space and Technology (now the Committee on Science), calls for a new social compact between scientists and society.[28] Barbara Mikulski, Brown's former counterpart in the Senate, asks that American scientists present their

---

[25] All quotations in this paragraph come from personal communications to the authors.

[26] David Goodstein, "Scientific Elites," p. 23.

[27] For the experiences of British scientists circa the early 1980s, see John Ziman, *Knowing Everything About Nothing: Specialization and Change in Scientific Careers* (New York: Cambridge University Press, 1987).

[28] George E. Brown, Jr., "New Ways of Looking at U.S. Science and Technology," *Physics Today* (Sept. 1994): pp. 31-35.

research priorities in terms of some socially useful *strategy*.[29] In a climate of "reinvention" and "doing more with less," it is possible that future careers will call upon scientists to employ a constellation of skills not previously acknowledged by their mentors and their peers as legitimate or highly valued.

Any new social compact between science and society must change the way certain tasks in science are valued over others. Chemist and Radcliffe president Linda Wilson wants the science community to take the lead by recalibrating the values it has traditionally assigned to the various tasks of science. In a December 1991 address to the Government-Industry-University Research Roundtable of the National Academy of Sciences, Wilson joined the issue head on, calling for a "reexamination of the criteria or indicators of excellence, utility, and achievement in science."[30] In this address and others, she cites a whole range of tasks in science that don't get rewarded by scientists (and, as a result, sometimes don't get done) because, as she explained, breaking new ground is valued more than synthesis and consolidation of knowledge, discovery is valued more than transmission and application of knowledge, and so on down a list that, in her view, places public understanding of science and the ethics of science at the very bottom. Wilson's address drew blood in ensuing weeks after it appeared in print. Letters to the editor of a national science magazine accused her of undermining excellence (meaning discovery of new knowledge) by assigning value to other tasks of science.[31] But however unpalatable, Wilson's focus on *valuing* in science goes right to the heart of a shift under way as the old social compact gives way to the new, a shift between stale perceptions and emerging realities of science as a career.

From this perspective, Goodstein is not only right in 1995; he would have been right all along. There won't be, there can't be a research professorship for every aspiring Ph.D. in science—but not just because there is an oversupply of Ph.D.s. Rather, Ph.D.s were not all supposed to become professors in the first place. One way to explain the *size* of the pool of applicants for college and university positions and the intensity of young scientists' sense of betrayal in the face of the job short-

---

[29] Barbara Mikulski calls it "strategic science." Quoted in Boyce Rensberger, "Fundamental Research at Risk," Part III of the *Washington Post* series, "American Science: Losing its Cutting Edge?" (Dec. 27, 1994): p. A12. The entire article elaborates on this debate.

[30] Linda S. Wilson, "The Scientific Community at a Crossroads: Discovery in a Cultural and Political Context," NAS, unpublished, p. 10.

[31] Her critics' fear that "excellence" would be sacrificed to other criteria was also fueled by Wilson's insistence, in the same address, on a recruitment and reward system in science that would attract and accommodate more women and minorities. "Comments From Readers," *The Scientist* (Mar. 16, 1992): pp. 11, 13.

age is that they have not been prepared practically or psychologically for work outside the academy. The tragedy, revealed by responses to our applicant survey (chapter 4), is that they don't find this out until their training is complete and they confront a sluggish or completely indifferent job market.

Asking university professors to be clairvoyant is unfair. Nobody knows how the "new social compact" between science and society will play itself out. But the signals so far don't bear out the professoriate's worst fears, namely, that the compact will abandon basic research. In a 1994 policy memorandum prepared by the National Science and Technology Council (NSTC), the Executive Office of Science and Technology Policy called on Congress to appropriate more, not less, of total federal R&D for *basic* research, to increase the share to universities, and to subject more of the government's R&D spending to peer review—all elements of the previous social compact.[32] At the same time, a certain percentage of every federal agency research budget has to be allocated to private enterprise, indicating a potential shift of at least some research dollars to the private sector.

Thus, a downturn in the growth rate of university science may signal the "end of a frontier," but not necessarily the end or even the beginning of the end of American science. What's good for university science was presumed for a long time to be good for American science, the economy, and national security, all rolled into one. That simple formula may have to go the way of Charley Wilson's much maligned "What's good for General Motors is good for America." University scientists owe it to their students to prepare them to cope with new challenges in new settings where they can experience the same satisfaction in more directly serving science and society that their professors found in doing academic science in an earlier era.

---

[32] *Science in the National Interest*, position paper produced by the Office of Science and Technology, Executive Office of the President, reported in *Nature* 389 (Jun. 1994): p. 34.

3

Report from the Field I

SCIENTISTS IN MIDCAREER

UNTIL very recently most scientists talked about science as if it were still an avocational pursuit of seventeenth-century gentlemen. Today leading academic scientists describe their careers as full of relentless pressures to win federal funding for research, to stave off institutional uncertainty, and to meet (or at least understand) public expectations. Life appears to be changing for industrial scientists as well. The breakup of AT&T in the 1970s, which took its toll on Bell Labs, and the downsizing of IBM and many chemical companies in the 1980s,[1] signaled the foreclosure of what was termed a "golden womb" for some industrial researchers.[2] What are the realities of a career in science today?

To answer this question, the authors distributed a lengthy "Career Questionnaire" to scientists in the first quarter of 1993 through Research Corporation's mailing list and acquaintances nationwide. Given resources and the scope of our work, we recognized that there was no way a group of three, working alone, could tap a statistically significant sample of the 30,000 Ph.D. physicists or 200,000 chemists currently employed. Our goal was to try, by means of "purposive" sampling, to identify trends among practicing scientists in academe and industry.[3] A reluctance by many to respond to the questionnaire, despite the cooperation of certain academic departments and managers at Pfizer, Rohm and Haas, Miles Laboratories, and Schlumberger, led us to augment our response by tapping the entire B.A.-B.S. graduate pool in physics and

---

[1] One exception is the pharmaceuticals. See special section, "Employment in the U.S. Chemical Industry," *Chemical and Engineering News* (Jul. 4, 1994): pp. 54-57.

[2] The term "golden womb" is attributed to researchers by James Hughes, an economist at Rutgers University, quoted by Tom Redburn, "Research Alley Adds New Life with Spinoffs," *New York Times* (Aug. 15, 1994): p. A1.

[3] Omitted altogether were scientists working for the federal government—an omission for which we were chastised by certain of our own respondents.

astronomy from the University of Nebraska and Carleton College, and
graduates in chemistry from Mount Holyoke College.[4]

Five areas of inquiry were selected: (1) influences on, and preparation for a career in science; (2) satisfaction; (3) perception of opportunities, barriers, and obstacles; (4) policy awareness—respondents'
prescriptions for the future; and, (5) planned and unplanned changes
that had taken place along the career path. We also inquired about the
part played by social institutions (graduate programs, postdoctoral experience, mentors, and family) in furthering informants' career development. How did key people and organizations assist or deter the at-
tainment of career goals? Respondents offered us wonderful texture
and rare insights—the kind of self-analysis that captures both career-
shaping motivations and aspirations and transforms experience into prescriptions for improving the training and utilization of scientists. Limited as the sample is, observations by science practitioners move us
beyond conventional survey data into the doubts and misgivings, and
the joys and accomplishments, that characterize a career in science.

Initially, we hoped to send out a special questionnaire to Ph.D.s who
had launched careers in physical science and had switched to other
kinds of employment, partly because we believe there will be more of
these in the future. We located a number of managers among our small
sample of industrial scientists, but had no way of judging whether these
men and women were still practicing science. There's a strong view in
the subculture of science that once one has stepped away from the
laboratory bench or, for the theoretician, the computer and the blackboard, one is no longer a scientist. But apart from such nomenclature
and self-identification issues, it was all but impossible to locate "switchers" with a survey. By definition, they had moved out of the traditional
areas in which scientists are employed and into other realms.[5]

We learn from what follows that because talent is made so much of
in science—as one of our respondents put it, "it's all on the test and the
test never ends"—careers in science are especially subject to human
expectations, misgivings, and disappointment, both in oneself and in
others.[6] But if science is not now what it once was, it is also not yet

[4] See Appendix for the various questionnaires sent to all four groups—"Career," "Industry,"
"Graduate," and "Applicant"—and for the inquiries sent over the Young Scientists' Network. The
Nebraska graduates included some who later got their Ph.D.s from the University of Nebraska.

[5] Anecdotal information abounds. See for example, "Washington Science Writer Is Former Bio-
psychologist: An Insider's View of Science and the Media," *American Psychological Society Observer* (May 1991): pp. 23-25. But formal survey data of the kind that will quantify how scientists
use their training in other fields is only now beginning to be collected. In 1994-95, too late for
inclusion in this book, the AIP surveyed the members of Sigma Pi Sigma, the physics honorary
society. Results show the size and nature of the "switcher" pool among that cohort.

[6] Such stress is not limited to science. Careers in medicine, law, and arts are similarly competitive.

what it is going to be. As the twentieth century wanes, certain changes are already noticeable. For one thing—and the younger scientists know this better than their mentors—science is populated by both genders; for another, scientists are already working in more sectors of the economy, engaged in a wider variety of activities in addition to research, doing much of their work with computers and communicating via Internet, and are more likely to be team members rather than individual researchers. The realities of today's science have rendered obsolete the stereotypes of an earlier era. It is time that we catch up with the psyche, as well as the perceptions, of the modern American scientist.

Collective Biography

Given the nature of our sampling technique ("purposive" as against random), there was no way that we could generalize about today's practitioner. What we aimed for, rather, is what historians call "collective biography" based on self-reporting. Self-reporting has much to offer. For example, the voluble responses from our 85 practicing scientists (the first solicitation) showed an obvious dichotomy traceable to respondents' positions in either academe or industry. We originally sent out a single questionnaire, but soon added additional questions ("Industry Questionnaire") designed for industrial employees. The reason was that scientists in the private sector were annoyed (and let us know) at having to fill out one more questionnaire that favored or assumed academic employment. Industrial scientists consider themselves different, and there was more than a hint in their responses that they were tired of questions that treated them as if they were in some way failed academics. With most professional chemists engaged in industry and a growing number of physicists seeking work in the private sector, they were anything but that. (For analysis of our industrial respondents, see "Industrial Scientists," page 50 ff.)

From the initial Career Questionnaire, all but 15 of 84 respondents hold Ph.D.s. Their age is normally distributed, with the median falling in the 45-49 range; the median year of their highest degree falls in the late 1970s. The second sample ("Graduate") is larger and, because it tapped entire B.A. and B.S. graduate populations of Carleton College and the University of Nebraska in physics, and the entire graduate population in chemistry of Mount Holyoke College, it can be categorized by age cohorts, which turns out to be highly revealing.[7] Indeed, once we eliminated the Mount Holyoke chemistry majors who had studied medicine after college or had not worked in science (69 out of 204),

---

[7] The departments of physics at University of Nebraska and Carleton College added our questionnaire to their annual alumni letter in academic year 1993-1994.

we found few gender-related differences between Mount Holyoke's female chemistry graduates and Nebraska's and Carleton's largely male graduates in physics and physics-astronomy (150 males, 22 females) in "satisfaction" with their careers, "reasons for choosing and staying in science," "influences on career choice," and "whether the U.S. needs more scientists." By far, the greater disparities occur among age cohorts.

Gender may be diminishing as a difference variable among these high achievers, but it still acts like a prism to refract careers. We could easily write separate narratives around the careers of men versus women. We have chosen not to do so, but many of the quotations below suggest that gender influences how both sexes see the world and their place in it. Culture reinforces these differences. Many women respondents talk about this in their answers to our questions. Another distinction must be drawn between industrial and academic careers. Despite the sameness of the training, the differences in experience and outlook are substantial, even though, in our sample, neither academics nor industrial scientists were "pure"—as many as 25 percent of our industrial scientists had academic experience, and slightly fewer academics had industrial experience. It was our task to tease out perceptions of their profession held by these science-trained individuals.

Of the 172 total respondents to our solicitation of Nebraska and Carleton graduates, 88 now have Ph.D.s, 39 M.S. degrees, 2 are physicians, 4 hold M.B.A. degrees, and 1 is a lawyer.[8] The working scientists are distributed over physics, aeronautics, astronomy, atmospheric science, business, engineering, electrical engineering, environmental science, and history of science. Thirty-two are under 30; 42 are in the 30-39 age bracket; 36 in the 40-49 age bracket; 38 are between 50 and 59, and 24 are over 60. Of the physics and physics-astronomy majors from Nebraska and Carleton, a larger percentage by far went on for Ph.D.s (88 out of 172) than among the Mount Holyoke chemistry majors (58 out of 204).

Influences on, and preparation for, a career in science

Influences on the choice of career among men showed "family" to be not much higher in importance than among women, and "school" and "social issues" to be about the same. However, there were significant differences by age in the scientists' descriptions of themselves as "recruited" to their career in science, or having had a career that was "unplanned." A substantial number of physics Ph.D.s in the 40-49 age group indicated that they had been recruited to their career. In no other age group was this a factor—again reflecting the period twenty to thirty years ago when physics was on a high growth curve. As for

---

[8] The age distribution was about the same in both samples.

"reasons for taking your current job," "opportunities for learning" was as much a factor with men as with women. "Quality of coworkers," "location," and "job security" were close seconds, but "spouse's wishes" among this overwhelmingly male population figured very low—in all age ranges.

It is important that a person's career is seen in the full context of family, geography, and salary, among other factors. Yet, the comments we received focus more on the individuated self, on what made science interesting, important, and accessible to a particular respondent, especially in the early years. Variations on the following appear with some frequency: "The space program galvanized an entire generation of young scientists and engineers"; [A50][9] "I am convinced that a classical liberal arts education is the best preparation for scientists"; [A22] "My research professor had come to academe from industry, so he told me about industry"; [A65] "My math skills were good enough for chemistry and not good enough for physics, so I made the right choice there." [A39] For women, the variable was often a special set of experiences, such as this one: ". . . the time [spent] helping my uncle, as his girl Friday, working at 'male' jobs with my hands." [A37]

The Career Questionnaire (with the Industry and Graduate versions) gathered a full array of responses to the question of whether, from the respondents' point of view, science is a calling. Answers ranged from "this is nonsense" to "I never thought of it that way" and "I guess so." The question seemed to strike a chord, one way or the other. Some were clearly comfortable with the notion that theirs had been a natural aptitude or a true interest. One, however, thought the attitude that science has to be a calling "functions as a way of excluding people from science who don't have the proper obsession." [A96]

Satisfaction

What do practitioners equate with satisfaction? Assuming this is a career goal, we were most curious about the responses. Would they be idealistic and abstract, or concrete and outcome-oriented? Unlike their reasons for getting into science, work satisfaction hinges very much on variables outside the respondents' control. In answer to the question "How would you rate your overall satisfaction with your career?" a majority of the Mount Holyoke chemists who were either under 30 or over 50 were "very satisfied" or "satisfied enough to do it again." Less positive was the 30-39 age group.[10] Only the under-30s in the total

---

[9] Numbers in brackets refer to specific questionnaire responses. To preserve anonymity, questionnaires were coded by number upon receipt and later archived.

[10] Eighty-seven of the chemistry majors (41%) ended up in chemistry as a career; 25 (12%) ended up in biochemistry, and a scattering found work in pharmacology, oceanography, industrial health, industrial engineering, molecular biology, environmental science, and computer science.

sample showed a level of disappointment of 18%, with highest satisfaction indicated by the over-60s closely followed by those ten and twenty years younger. One can postulate that some of those under 30 are still in graduate school and have not yet encountered the job crunch or the infamous glass ceiling that awaits women in certain job settings. Those over 50 have spent much of their career during a "golden age" of science.

Answers to the open-ended questions revealed how much external circumstances influence career satisfaction.

> Our school is very poor and when the economy is bad we all suffer and morale declines. If the president or dean is an SOB, satisfaction diminishes. If my students are victims of shoddy high school education, my classes are reminiscent of the labors of Sisyphus. [A81]

> [My] immediate environment is far more important than national funding trends, etc. [A33]

Another respondent complained about the threat of "fundamentalist, anti-intellectual, or bottom-line, short-term attitudes . . . [that] diminish opportunity [and] waste time." [A60] For the younger scientists, the final balance is yet to be drawn:

> I was given the impression there would always be jobs. . . . If I do not get tenure at my current job, I may feel very differently. [A44]

> The economy dictates the state of funding. This low level of funding has negatively impacted my career. [A108]

From one respondent comes a comment reminiscent of Daniel Koshland's prescription (see page 11)—namely, that a scientist needs, in addition to everything else, a job.

> I'm in science because I like it, and I've liked it since my childhood. I'm not in it to get rich, but if it couldn't support a reasonable life style I'd get out. [A55]

Do they see themselves as typical? This question says something about how representative our purposively selected sample is, as volunteered by respondents. Remember that by most measures these are successful scientists. They have jobs, accomplishments, and fond recollections of why they chose science as a career. Among the Mount Holyoke alumnae, there were discrepancies concerning their perceptions, as women and as scientists, of how typical they were among others of their age group and gender. Not surprisingly, those over 60 thought of themselves as least typical (17%), those under 30 as most typical, and the intermediate age groups showed a great many more "don't knows." This confirms our sense of how very much a career in science is considered acceptable for women today. The Carleton and Nebraska physics majors (mostly male) answered similarly across all age groups, except for those 40-49, some 40% of whom considered themselves a little less typical (we don't know why). The others were much less conscious of being different from their peers.

Opportunities, barriers and obstacles

We get important insights into opportunities, barriers, and obstacles, both from the questions directed to those issues and from responses to the open-ended question about advice respondents would give to the next generation. These answers are transparently personal, some full of rancor, some more idealistic like one respondent's injunction, "Touch the future: teach." [A2]

> It's shocking how competitive and ruthless other scientists can be. I've had more encouragement as a fiction writer than I've had as a scientist. [A31]

> I would warn about peer pressure that constrains creativity. [A58]

Asked their reasons for taking current positions, Mount Holyoke women scientists identified location as very important—more important than spouse's job opportunities—although "location" may have masked concern for spouse and family. But the influence of partners and spouses on the success or failure of careers of younger scientists was evident among younger male scientists as well. This shows up in comments, such as: "Wife wanted relocation to her hometown." [A17]

"Opportunity for advancement" ranked low (19%) among the women chemists, compared to "opportunity for learning" (67%), and "quality of coworkers" ranked higher than "salary." This last could well be a reflection of the upper-class origins of these Mount Holyoke graduates and the fact that, as married women, theirs was a second family income. Striking among all age groups in the Mount Holyoke sample was how important "school" and "social issues" were in directing them to careers in science. (Those who chose medicine were similarly motivated.) "Family influence" showed up as a lesser factor in all but the 40-49 age group and the over-60s, which may be their way of implying that the family was unsupportive. But males in our sample got surprisingly little family support as well. On "social issues" all age groups among the women were more alike than they were different: the over-60s gave "social issues" a 43% weighting in the factors that impelled them to science; the 30-50 year olds 63%, and the youngest cohort 46%.

Negative mentoring is a factor for men as well as women. If older male scientists sometimes disparage or ignore the strengths and skills of their female students (as was reported by some women chemists), they can also respond more punitively to the "threats" posed by younger males. But "bad mentors" were not seen as malevolent by our graduates, just not very useful. And for those who went on to earn a Ph.D., the postdoc experience didn't always achieve the young scientist's goals. For some, it provided a painful entry into the real world of science.

> The [two] postdoc positions I held were not aimed at scientific research per se but rather at making enough noise to convince funding agencies that good research was being done, or making a big PR splash for my mentor's own aggrandizement. [A133]

Policy awareness: respondents' prescriptions for the future

The respondents do not claim to be well informed about federal policies that impinge upon science and technology; a little less than half answered these questions. They are forthcoming in their descriptions of their situations, but hesitant or unable to prescribe what ought to be done about such problems as "training people for nonexistent jobs," "universities that are oblivious to market forces," and the "neglect of technology," particularly in academic institutions. [A40, A51] Most believe that more must be done to disabuse key players, both in and out of science, of wrong notions about the nature and utility of science. They are concerned about the ratio of foreign citizens to U.S. students in the nation's graduate schools; looking to the future, some wonder why "we don't have as many people of color and women succeeding in science as we have coming from other countries." [A91] In some cases, descriptions of the problem go deeper. One respondent notes, for example, that we in this country are better at "moving wealth and knowledge around [what M.B.A.s and lawyers do, as he sees it] than at generating new wealth and knowledge, the function of scientists and engineers." [A14] But he doesn't speculate as to why.

Respondents—particularly those who are working in industry—see much to criticize in the "academic model." For one, "it sacrifices too much talent in the search for superior quality." [A48] Another feels that scientists are being squeezed onto "narrow tracks which suit few, employ few, and indoctrinate others to see failure" in being anything except an academic. [A158] While one respondent sees too little attention being paid by academic scientists to market forces, another sees too much. "The effect of market forces," he writes, "has been to turn us into cannibals." [A57] Most believe the world has changed since their own education was completed. Some see this firsthand through in-school interactions with K-12 education, or with their children's teachers. Others have a generalized set of misgivings about American values and a widening gap between the "Two Cultures."[11]

> I am worried. There are not enough scientists being trained, but more than that, those who are being trained are deficient in the liberal arts . . . . They are ignorant about the social, cultural, and human context of their work. And they are not effective agents of needed change. [A188]

> U.S. science is elitist, narrow, closed to change. Until science becomes willing to allow alternative approaches for thinking about . . . nature, the prospects seem bleak. Physics [may be] on its way out, like classical Greek. [A150]

In answer to whether the U.S. needs more science and engineering talent in industry, government, universities, or in primary and secondary school education, the "more in universities" column attracted the fewest "yes" responses (42% among the Mount Holyoke chemistry graduates, 23% among the Carleton and Nebraska physics graduates). Those under 30 were less inclined to see a shortage. The industry category attracted the largest number of "yes" responses (70% among the Mount Holyoke chemistry graduates, 78% among the Carleton and Nebraska physics graduates who answered this question). And, although they themselves had not gone into K-12 teaching, all but the under-30s thought primary-secondary education needed science-trained personnel most of all (69% among the Mount Holyoke chemistry graduates, 65% among the Carleton and Nebraska physics graduates).

In short, when it comes to questions about the future or about public policy, hand-wringing and good intentions abound, but alternative modes, either of educating future scientists or of providing them with opportunities for continuous employment, are lacking. Perhaps it's because our respondents, in general, find politicians "uneducable" and indifferent to science. Faced with the daunting task of arguing in Congress for additional research funding or of having to allocate dollars by discipline and project, however, it is not clear that those who complain would welcome the opportunity, or do a better job if they were in charge.

---

[11] Referring to the phrase made famous by C.P. Snow, *The Two Cultures and A Second Look* (Cambridge, U.K.: Cambridge University Press, 1964).

Such is today's academic practitioner. Respondents have few regrets personally. Though they are critical of the organization and structure of science, they are remarkably passive in the face of change. Perhaps it is because they—the younger scientists more than the older ones—feel out of control of the future of science in America and no less of their own destiny.

Industrial Scientists

Our "Industry Questionnaire," mailed out by cooperating managers, allowed us to tap into the pool of science-trained professionals working in large industrial R&D laboratories. As compared to academic scientists, the sixty-eight scientists in industry who sent back usable responses lead decidedly distinctive work lives. Their work rewards different sets of skills and it is clear that different motivations drive them. Although efficiency is supposed to prevail in the private sector, we glean from our respondents' comments that the fit between individual career aspirations and the needs of the organization is not always a good one.

In all, our industrial informants augmented what we learned from academic practitioners and from job-seeking neophytes (see chapter 4). Collectively, the industry sample was 59% male and in their mid-to-late 40s. Of the highest degrees, 67% were earned in chemistry; 85% of our industry respondents possess Ph.D.s. Two out of three had but a single job through most of their science career, and 10% have had just two. Their comments can be grouped into five categories: (1) professional life skills; (2) career origins; (3) career satisfaction; (4) personal and institutional change; and (5) responsibility for improving what might be called the "big picture."

Professional life skills

Many responses to the question, "What skills derived from your scientific training have proved to be most valuable throughout your career?" are notable. They go beyond anticipated answers—experimental design, scientific method, problem solving—and stress seldom articulated life skills. "Versatility! Knowing how to apply techniques and principles to new areas of research," writes one respondent. [A77] Another says, ". . . not being afraid to ask for help when you don't understand." [9] Valuable skills for others are more specific: computer usage; data-based decision making; written and oral communication skills; work ethic and persistence; the ability to ask questions, to reason, to work as a team member; and organization and planning. Some fewer mention life lessons, such as "the realization that you have to foster your own career." [A101]

Career origins: A calling to science?

When we asked our industrial scientists whether they thought the "calling" explanation applied to them, a divergence of opinion emerged from "yes" to "no" to "let's rethink and relabel this." [A7] One wrote of the calling explanation: "Not a bad description. I certainly didn't know very much about what 'real scientists' do when I made the decision [to pursue science]." [A201] Others put it differently: "If doing what you like and are good at is being 'called,' I was." [5] "Science felt to me like my manifest destiny." [21] "There's something to this," wrote a third. "I might call it more a 'predisposition' than a 'calling'. . . . " [8] Another wisely notes that when a child's "predisposition" gets a lot of positive reinforcement, it may be interpreted as a calling. He recollects as follows: "'Calling' is probably another word for what happened to me. You start getting rewards and praise for one subject, so you decide to [pursue] it." [43]

Other professionals cite different factors, such as the one who wrote, "I found a variety of sciences interesting and it seemed a profession that paid well." [12] Or, more strongly, "I never felt called and I still don't. If I could earn this much money doing volunteer work, I'd switch today because I get even more satisfaction from it than from chemistry." [26] And for a few, the term "calling" seems quaint, appropriate to an earlier era. One thinks the idea of a calling is "probably not relevant in today's world, but that's the way I felt growing up." [A195]

So far, the industrial scientists are not much different from the academic practitioners. But, threaded throughout their responses to our questionnaire (though not mentioned as frequently by academic respondents) are references to their collective fascination with expertise and technical knowledge. One remembers as a young person admiring scientists for their understanding of subjects not understood by laymen. Another never viewed science as "mystical:" "Instead, I was always interested in how things worked and how to make stuff. I was attracted to science, not called to it." [A122]

Who gets satisfaction?

Several questions related to the subject of career satisfaction: overall "satisfaction" rating for career, factors relevant to career satisfaction; the importance of an immediate supervisor to satisfaction; and whether or not the respondent would major in science now if given the opportunity to choose. Many of our industrial informants noted the key role of the "boss" in career satisfaction—the personality and management style of one's immediate supervisor. Another theme that recurs is the need for freedom and "space to be creative," as does satisfaction from managing and completing a project. [18]

Whether to proceed into management is often mentioned as a critical issue by industrial scientists. On the one hand, there is the satisfaction of managing and completing a project, which sometimes is muted when one has overall responsibility for many. There is more opportunity, more power, and, above all, more money in management. On the other hand, there is the palpable loss of the bench. Many respondents offered that "management can make or break your career," meaning not just how well the scientist's own work is managed, but whether or not he or she decides to move up. "To use science as a stepping stone to something else (like upper management)," writes one respondent, "will only lead to disappointment." [A66] "The money is better, but it doesn't compensate for what is lost." [19][12]

Industry respondents (to a larger extent than academics) find that satisfaction depends on the state of the economy and on "the personal views of the board of directors." [31] "It's nice to be able to write a requisition for a new instrument and have it delivered the next month," one woman working in a pharmaceutical company told us in a follow-up interview, "instead of having to wait a year or more for a project involving that instrument to be funded." [A80] But a failed lawsuit or a marketing decision can destroy an entire project, eliminate an entire division. The point is and was made often by our industrial respondents: Survival in a business environment involves politics and interpersonal relations, factors outside even a manager's control. While quality of work is important, it is insufficient to win or keep a job that guarantees intellectual satisfaction and professional security, attributes highly valued by both industrial and academic scientists.

Changing jobs

Why do industrial scientists change jobs? Conventional wisdom holds that for every career move there are both push and pull factors. The grass may appear greener on the other side of the fence, but on entering the neighboring yard the brown spots and the weeds are revealed. Combine this allure with the increasing insecurity of aging professionals, and push and pull can be very real. Our industrial informants display a range of attitudes toward change in their own careers. Some are buried deep in the bowels of their companies and have neither need nor hope for change. Others grasp the bigger picture and reflect poignantly on organizational opportunities, obstacles, and the professional growth that has been fostered or blunted. Individual differences are prominent here, too. People have varying thresholds for dissatisfaction, hence varying

---

[12] An exception to our respondents' experience that upward mobility in industry involves "leaving science" is provided by Rohm and Haas. See "A Postscript from Industry," p. 55.

thresholds for change. With the streamlining of the industrial work force, globally as well as domestically, the security of corporate employment is no longer as certain as it once was. And our respondents know very well they may have to change careers as well as jobs, whether they want to or not.

Not all change is threatening. Among our responses are glimmers of real interest and pleasure in change: "I have been asked to change fields several times," writes one respondent. "And it has [always] been stimulating. International travel and working with people of other cultures has made me grow emotionally and intellectually." [A70] But all of our respondents are aware that their companies will be making marketing decisions that will affect their careers. "My changes within industry," writes one, "have been pushed by managerial changes in research focus as well as my desire to move up." [A111] These scientists are in the eye of the current economic storm. Can they ride out the upheaval or are they eyeing work in another sector? If there are more attractive alternatives, will their science training be adaptable in new settings? Or, will they have to retrain?

Implications for graduate education

Because respondents are aware that all fields of study are changing rapidly, they feel they must have the widest possible background—in effect, a skills bank—in order to compete. In thinking back on their own graduate training, they regret that flexibility wasn't emphasized more. They recognize, to quote one respondent, that "universities aren't cops . . . [they] can't force people to make sure their skills are transferable." [17] But they think graduation requirements should be stiffer and the point should be made again and again to young people that being educated means, more than anything else, being able to transfer, not just discover, new knowledge.

One avenue closed to industrial scientists (quite as much as to academic scientists, at least as they perceive it) is self-employment due to the cost of equipment and the difficulty for an unaffiliated scientist of raising venture capital or getting nonprofit funding. Very few of our respondents were self-employed.[13] (This also has to do with the authors' inability to find a way to locate the self-employed.) Several scientists spoke with more than a little longing of self-employment, and a num-

---

[13] Too late for inclusion in this book we came across a letter from Helen Gourley, an optical scientist with the System Sciences Group of San Francisco, to the APS Committee on the Status of Women in Physics which describes a course she teaches for scientists and engineers in industry called "switching from employee to consultant." For a similar view, see Catherine Reed, "To Jobless Scientists: Don't Give Up . . . You *Can* Pursue Your Research," *The Scientist* (May 3, 1993): p. 11.

ber of women respondents chided us for not including questions in our survey about flex-time, part-time, or job-sharing options within science careers.

Policy awareness: respondents' prescriptions for change

Industrial scientists appear more realistic and policy-wise than their academic counterparts. Perhaps it is because they work within profit-making companies that pay attention to the bottom line that they are more willing than university practitioners to think about relationships between supply and demand for people as well as products. They note that while universities turn out employable scientists in a pretty steady stream, hiring itself is cyclical. "Some years good people can't get jobs," writes one respondent. "Other years mediocre people get many offers." [2] How to align supply with demand is the kind of concern industrial scientists will articulate. They don't have government funding agencies to blame for a lack of jobs. Even those who are not concerned about their own immediate futures ("I'm not worried. The cultural and financial bases are solid," wrote one) express concern about "government and business leaders who are not scientifically literate." [7] One gets the impression that many industrial scientists have experienced first-hand the effects of scientific illiteracy on business decisions.

While their descriptions of the problem appear to be more sophisticated, or at least couched in terms closer to those of a policy analyst than those proffered by our academic respondents, industrial scientists offer no real prescriptions for change. Their ideas on the subject are limited to increased funding for graduate education and ways of correcting what they see as the image of scientists in popular culture.

Conclusion

If change in the training and counseling of the next generation of scientists is understood as necessary by both academic and industrial practitioners, who will be in charge? Who should implement change? Are the roles assigned to university, government, and industry in preparing new scientists appropriately delineated? Or, as some of our industrial informants believe, are these institutions failing the next generation in not doing long-term planning?

For scientists employed in industry and business, science is both a social and cultural good and a potential source of America's economic revitalization. It is also a personal adventure. While few originally imagined themselves working in the private sector, that's where they are, and given the scarcity of jobs in academe, that's where they will remain. Rare is the industrial scientist who, like the IBM vice president who recently retired, can go to the University of Virginia as an adjunct professor; or the platinum chemist whose division was eliminated and who found a teaching position at a state university. To the extent there are any pathways between academe and industry, they tend to be one-way streets. Still, industrial scientists have much to contribute to our collective thinking about the future of science, about training the next generation, and about understanding the vicissitudes of supply and demand.

A Postscript from Industry

Not every chemical industry lab is as productive or attached to as prosperous a company as that in Spring House, Pennsylvania, corporate research headquarters for Rohm and Haas. With net sales of over $3 billion a year, the firm's annual report makes it quite clear how much research and development is valued. Research claims about $205 million (6% of sales), the highest percentage of research as a proportion of sales in nonpharmaceutical chemicals. Although sales at Rohm and Haas are distributed over several categories of chemicals, the company leads the world in the production of emulsion polymers.[14] The Spring House "campus" is a collection of buildings in a rural setting, and houses 400 Ph.D.s, mostly chemists, some chemical engineers, biochemists and biologists, and 700 other employees holding high school, baccalaureate, or master's degrees.

In some ways Rohm and Haas is typical. More than 80 percent of trained chemists who go to work in industry work for chemical companies like Rohm and Haas, Miles, Monsanto, and American Cyanamid; only 20 percent are employed by the pharmaceutical industry. Yet, pharmaceutical companies, according to a Rohm and Haas senior chemist interviewed for this book, have a higher status among university chemists. "My senior professor," she said, "was disappointed when I went to a chemical company. 'I didn't spend five years of my life training you to work in a chemical company,' he told me. The reason for his attitude? Pharmaceutical research is considered more complex and therefore more elegant—small versus large molecules—and hence higher in status."

In the 1980s Rohm and Haas took steps to improve its career ladders for scientists. To solve the problem of their having to move into

[14] The company's products are distributed unequally among agricultural chemicals ($409 million in sales); plastics ($579 million); performance chemicals ($762 million); and polymers, resins, and monomers ($1.5 billion). All figures come from financial highlights, Rohm and Haas 1993 annual report.

management to get ahead—a complaint our respondents reiterate—
the company has created three positions on the technical ladder:
"research fellow," equivalent in salary and status to first line research
management; "senior research fellow," equivalent to middle research
management; and "corporate research fellow," equivalent to upper
research management. This satisfies the industrial scientist who wants
to keep working at the bench. But Jim Burke, manager of research
staffing who follows trends in the hiring of chemists nationally, thinks
we still have a long way to go in changing academic attitudes. Many
professors, he says, still want their "best 10 percent" to go into university teaching, and the next best 20 percent are encouraged to
enter college teaching. Industry is considered appropriate only for
the lower 70 percent.[15]

Attitude is part of the problem, says Burke, funding for graduate
education another. There are fewer and fewer fellowships that graduate students can take with them, and fewer and fewer block grants
awarded to universities. Of the first-year graduate students in chemistry in 1961, he tells us, eighty held NSF predoctoral fellowships. In
1994, with the same total number of U.S. citizens beginning graduate
programs in chemistry, only fifteen held such fellowships. Fellowships and block grants took much of the fund-raising burden off faculty, and more importantly, according to Burke, "faculty had more
time to devote to mentoring graduate students, enabling them to
become more independent of their senior professors, able to design
their own research projects and to set some distance from their adviser—just what industry is looking for."[16]

Burke is also critical of a general attitude among educators toward technicians. "We need to stop thinking about technicians as a
pair of hands," he says. On the one hand, he is eager to get Rohm and
Haas to hire more baccalaureate degree holders in chemistry and to
provide better technical career ladders for them. On the other, he
wants to institute a system of job levels based not on degrees, but on
competencies. The establishment in 1994 of a new Division of Chemical Technicians at the American Chemical Society, he says, is a step
in the right direction. "Your degree," he commented, "should determine your entry level, not where you end up."

Some scientists at the company do proceed into management, but
only because they want to and are willing to retrain. Ph.D. chemist
Ann Beaulieu enrolled in the nearby Wharton School of Business to
earn a two-year certificate including courses in business law, account-

---

[15] Jim Burke, personal communication to the authors.

[16] Ibid. What Burke calls a "block grant" is officially known as a "traineeship" awarded
to the institution to support graduate students as it seems appropriate.

ing, operations, labor relations, and organizational theory and behavior. She now holds an important administrative position with Rohm and Haas. According to Curt Mathews, manager of research personnel services at the company, "Beaulieu represents the future of industrial science." He thinks of her as a "gold-collar worker," a term now coming into parlance in the science industries, someone with three or more distinct areas of expertise. "Before, the 'best person' in a technical area would be offered the position of manager," Mathews explains. "In today's flattening managerial system, managers have to be even more broadly educated and trained."[17]

[17] Curt Mathews, personal communication to the authors.

A Postscript from the Government Sector

Work life at the nation's newest national laboratory, the Continuous Beam Electron Accelerator Facility (CEBAF) in Newport News, Virginia, is not like life at Los Alamos, Sandia, Lawrence Livermore, Hanford, or Oak Ridge. The Big Five were initially constructed largely to serve the military's nuclear needs, and currently employ tens of thousands of scientists. Since the national labs are now struggling to find new missions in a post-cold war environment, the authors thought it useful to spend time at one that was not primarily associated with weapons development and testing. Also of interest was meeting scientists doing "big science."

CEBAF is not yet finished. Seven years in construction, it is being commissioned and is due to come on line late in 1995. With a $700 million annual budget to build the facility, it will be considerably smaller and less ambitious than the Big Five. While there is mention of eventual practical applications arising from accelerator design and instrumentation, CEBAF is essentially dedicated, as one of the scientists put it, to studying "the sociology of the nucleus," by which he means the many-body interactions of nucleons. Even though careers at CEBAF are of recent origin, the facility is governed under the same rules as the other national labs. Wondering if the career experience of CEBAF scientists would be comparable, we arranged an informal meeting with a few.

What's the best thing about working in a national lab, compared to academe or industry? we asked. The answers ranged from "no teach-

ing" to "being able to work on instrumentation and not just take data."
One informant explained that nontheoretical research among university scientists is very often constrained by what is recognized as
valuable.[18] What he is working on, he insists, is vital to science, extremely exciting and satisfying to himself, but would be difficult to
do if he were competing for promotion in a university setting. As far
as job security is concerned, CEBAF workers hold long-term contracts dependent on continued government funding, which makes
them somewhat dependent on congressional whim. Then again, as
one said, state universities are dependent on state legislatures and
boards of regents. There individual research projects are even more
unstable and the principal investigator has to raise his own funds.

However much our respondents distinguished between the national lab and university environments, they all came out of universities, and CEBAF has made it possible for them to enjoy a university-
like working atmosphere. There are seminars; postdocs and graduate
students; international visitors hosted at an "on campus" residence
facility; self-direction; and the same obsessive-compulsiveness about
work that scientists everywhere exhibit. Women are few but well-
respected, and married couples in the same field of physics, engineering, or computer science have a better chance of getting two
jobs at CEBAF than they would at even a large state university. "Best
of all," said one, "six of the top seven administrators of CEBAF have
Ph.D.s in science. You wouldn't find that at a university."

Although a couple of the people we spoke with had worked in
industry and said CEBAF was like industry in many ways, they were
eager to point out that it was also like a university, only better. They
won't make professor at a national lab, and even with a "senior" in
front of it, the title of staff scientist I, II, or III cannot compete for
lustre. But they seem content, enthusiastic, and very satisfied. And
the reasons were not hard to find. Even during a brief visit, the cama-
raderie among CEBAF scientists was evident. Like sailors on a single
ship or members of a cooperative, they are not in competition with
one another, since each is necessary to the various large-scale projects
they are working on. And since they are not each running projects or
teaching graduate students and postdocs, they have more time to be
intellectually engaged with each other. An unofficial "vision plaque"
posted in one office perhaps sums up life at CEBAF: "A fun place
where diverse, talented people spend their most creative years responsibly solving problems that enhance our understanding of the
universe and improve the way we live."

---

[18] According to a CEBAF administrator speaking with the authors, articles on instrumentation are not highly recognized or rewarded among academics.

4

Report from the Field II

TODAY'S PHYSICAL SCIENTIST AS JOB APPLICANT

Yesterday marked the one-year anniversary of my Ph.D. defense, and ordinarily that should have been cause for celebration. However, at this point I feel I have nothing to show for my hard work. Presently I am teaching one course at a community college an hour and a half's drive away, and when I divide what I'm being paid by the time I'm putting into this effort—not even counting the commute time—I find I'm barely making a minimum wage. Otherwise, I'm unemployed and filling up my time by taking care of two small children, finishing up some leftover research from my grad student days, and sending out job applications. My wife works full-time and makes a good salary, but I'd like a little more reward for all the hard work I've done the past many years than to sit at home and take care of kids . . . .

—Applicant Questionnaire from Las Cruces, New Mexico

THIS frustrated young Ph.D. did in fact have one post-degree job at a science museum in a town seventy-five miles from where he was living. When he took the job, he found his employment contract harbored a few "surprises": $10,000 less in pay than had been promised, no health benefits, few resources to carry out projects that had been discussed, and a required two-week *unpaid* vacation per year. After two and one-half months on that job, the scientist resigned.[1] It is always possible to dismiss a single example, and even many anecdotal

---

[1] Taken from a letter to the authors dated Mar. 5, 1993 .

accounts do not necessarily indicate a trend. The respondent could well have poor judgment, lack scientific ability or, because of his wife's career, not be as flexible as professionals of earlier generations. But his plight is by no means unique.

How does one go from anecdote to analysis? One way is to query a sample of all Ph.D. recipients in a particular field within five years of their doctorates. The difficulties of doing this (see chapter 1) are that many cannot be located or do not respond. Another way—one of the two we have chosen—is to query the job applicant. Job applicants are rarely studied, not just because they are hard to locate but because their status is considered temporary. Given the current decline in positions for scientists, however, job searching lasts longer and is fraught with uncertainty as to whether or not a professional position will ultimately be obtained. Indeed, by the spring of 1995, when this book was being completed, the National Research Council, NSF, and most of the major professional organizations were becoming aware that underemployment of the nation's science-trained personnel needed to be tracked quite as much as unemployment.

A third route to employment data is to seek patterns by "listening in" on conversation among job seekers—an opportunity afforded this writing team through the Young Scientists' Network (YSN), a 3,000-person electronic network for the unemployed or underemployed, founded by one of the authors. Although the YSN includes more people trained in physics than chemistry, many of the concerns and frustrations expressed on the network apply to people trained in any of the sciences.[2] It is all very well for author and physicist Peter Feibelman to advise young scientists to "apply the same brain power to planning their careers" as they do to their research, and not to "assume by investing your youth that you are entitled to a job."[3] But it is something else, in the absence of help with career planning, for graduates to be unexpectedly faced with the need to formulate job-hunting strategies on their own.

The Applicant Questionnaire

In an effort to put a human face on the unemployment statistics, four academic department chairs were asked to cooperate with the authors in the winter of 1993 in a survey of recently rejected applicants for

---

[2] See "Young Scientists' Network Provides Forum for Electronic Activism," *Physics Today* (May 1993): pp. 57-60; "Young Scientists' Network: group therapy for the frustrated," *Chemical and Engineering News* (Oct. 19, 1992): p. 26; Malcolm W. Browne, "Amid 'Shortage,' Young Physicists See Few Jobs," *The New York Times* (Feb. 20, 1994): p. A1; and Virginia Morell, "E-Mail Links Science's Young and Frustrated," *Science* 256 (1 May 1992): p. 606.

[3] Peter Feibelman, introduction to *A Ph.D. is not Enough: A Guide to Survival in Science* (Menlo Park, Calif.: Addison-Wesley, 1993).

faculty positions at their institutions. Two of the departments (in physics and astronomy) were located at Research I universities; and one in physics and the only one in chemistry were located at two selective liberal arts colleges.[4] We thought the departments' efforts to fill slots would have generated a typical sample of job applicants in a single year.[5] We asked the department chairs to send out over their own signatures hundreds of copies of the authors' "Applicant Questionnaire" (see Appendix, Section IV) to all those declined for a position. Despite their rejection (or perhaps because they were inured to being disappointed in job searches), the "failed applicants" responded very generously.[6]

The Applicant Questionnaire yielded 268 usable responses (out of a total mailing of approximately 750), and a dozen or so unsolicited long letters enlarging on some of the answers. The first subsample, from two searches (one in physics, one in physics and astronomy), yielded a population that was overwhelmingly male, born after 1950, all with the Ph.D. degree in hand. A later subsample culled from those applying for openings in chemistry as well as physics yielded a population one-quarter female and one-third chemists. Cover sheet information indicated that one-third of the respondents had been looking for a job in science for more than two years, with another quarter having searched between one and two years (the average for the entire sample was 18 months).

The bulk of the respondents to the Applicant Questionnaire were not yet employed, and some had been searching so long they needed to narrow the time frame to respond, answering the length-of-job-search question with pointed comments such as, "six months *this* year," and hints of longer periods if we considered the fact that present jobs were temporary. Others appended long personal letters describing a pattern of search-employment-search that was nowhere near an end. One respondent, a high-energy physicist with an undergraduate degree from Princeton and a graduate degree from Cornell, sent out 105 separate applications for his first postdoc (which yielded one offer) and 146 for his second (which yielded none). He calls this the "November ritual . . . [when] all research activity comes to a halt as we do our duty to keep the

---

[4] The institutions, respectively, were University of New Mexico, Michigan State University, Colorado College, and Macalester College.

[5] Since the departments did not keep a demographic record of their failed applicants, the authors are unable to ascertain whether the demographic make-up of the respondents is the same as that of the applicants.

[6] Owing to proprietary privilege, we did not get cooperation from industrial and commercial enterprises to do the same. As a result, our applicant pool consisted entirely of persons then looking for faculty positions. However, we did receive a great number of replies from scientists applying for postdocs in academic and national labs (see sections on postdoctoral appointments), many of whom were also on the industrial job market.

postal service profitable. The phone company benefits six months later when we do our follow-up calling." [161][7] Speaking for himself and a cohort in the same circumstances, he writes:

> We attempt to stay afloat (i.e., employed) from year to year, moving from postdoc to postdoc, while every fall we send out applications for faculty positions to any place that advertises, whether research university or small liberal arts college. As the years progress, it becomes more difficult for us to maintain our status as postdocs because we age both chronologically and professionally. If we do not obtain faculty positions after a certain length of time (I would estimate six to eight years as the absolute maximum) we are generally considered to be too old to be hired [either] as postdocs or professors.

Chemical and Engineering News told the story in October 1993 of a 31-year-old chemist in his fourth year of a postdoc that was only supposed to last two. "John" (he asked that his name be withheld), who in prior years would have had no trouble getting an academic position (according to his professors), holds a Ph.D. in inorganic materials chemistry from one of the top fifteen U.S. universities in terms of chemistry Ph.D.s granted, and is doing his postdoc at another of these institutions.[8] After sending out "highly tailored eighty-page packages of information" to sixty universities, John received few offers and watched funding difficulties foreclose several of the positions. He was unable to get a job better than his present postdoc, which he was able to extend. "You can't imagine the amount of time and money [looking for a job] costs," he says. Still, when *C&EN* interviewed him, he was hopeful that his next search would turn something up.

Few respondents are as sanguine. The dominant impression conveyed by our informants is that job searches have been bleak to "horrific." They express incredulity about the state of the market, surprise over the number of competitors for jobs (and over "the number of trees killed" for résumés), [38] anger about the insensitivity of various academic and industrial departments, and realism mixed with resignation about their long-term as well as short-term job prospects. Theirs is an amalgam of emotions that often includes a reassertion about why the respondent chose science, yet dismay ranging to bitterness over how

---

[7] Numbers in brackets refer to direct quotations from specific questionnaire responses. All questionnaires were coded by number to preserve anonymity and later archived. This respondent's group finally renewed his contract. Six months later he found another post at a more prestigious institution but not yet a long-term academic job.

[8] "New Chemistry Ph.D.s Face Sluggish Industrial, Academic Job Market," *Chemical and Engineering News* (Oct. 25, 1993): p. 45.

careers have been stillborn (a "horrifying realization that I might have spent seven years in graduate school for nothing"). [3]

The Search Process

The Applicant Questionnaire is a research tool designed to strip away the façade that most respondents would erect under other circumstances (direct interview or focus groups). In their responses to questions about the search process, recent job applicants are describing a less than happy time in their lives. After years of progress toward a degree under the eye of a senior professor, they are for the first time on their own, so much so that they are seriously questioning the directions their futures will take. Some, not surprisingly, feel cheated, bitter, or angry as well as frustrated (adjectives found repeatedly in responses). They also have much to tell us about what's wrong with a search process that is, even in good times, "unscientific," and in bad times, "sterile, anonymous, and Kafkaesque." [B7] Some informants were disoriented by the job quest. There was confusion over what hiring departments really wanted and, since rejection letters were unspecific, why in the end they didn't make the final cut. As more than one respondent expressed it, "Uncertainty [note he didn't say 'rejection'] eats away at your confidence and optimism." [120]

One way to sort out perceptions and realities in the job search process was to ask respondents why, in their opinion, they didn't get the jobs they applied for, and to compare their responses to the observations of department chairs and others. Some department administrators suspect that there are search services which, for a fee, collect help-wanted ads and provide job hunters with printouts. Applicants then use these lists to blanket hapless departments with mass-produced résumés and computer-generated cover letters. The reason for suspicion is the size and anomalies of the applicant pool. Ed Langer, chairman of physics at Colorado College, one of the departments hiring the year we did our survey, does not subscribe to the search-service theory but noticed that many of the job applicants held Ph.D.s from institutions from which the college does not usually recruit.[9] Another indication that some candidates are applying wholesale to more places than they can possibly be acquainted with came from a student member of a search committee at a women's college which advertised a position in physics a few years earlier. She also noted the sheer size and in many cases the inappropriateness of the applicant pool. "There were dozens," she reported, "who did not even know that they were applying to

---

[9] Ed Langer, personal communication to the authors.

a women's college or, if they did, made no mention of their particular commitment to the education of women."[10]

The perceptions of applicants, as opposed to employers, are vastly different. We received a wide range of answers to the question, "What were the reasons for not getting the job you applied for?" At least as important as the answers is the range of beliefs applicants harbor about the hiring process, and the degree to which they themselves are searching for explanations. As the display of their comments (see page 76) indicates, our applicants were not naive about themselves. Some conceded they were not well enough known professionally, that they wrote a weak cover letter, that their presentation was not lively enough; in short, that they were not the best applicant in the group.

Other problems, however, were more difficult to rationalize.[11] A mention during an interview that one applicant was considering an industrial job turned out to be a negative factor, as did another applicant's "unconventional background" (not specified). Personal contacts and the "grapevine" figure prominently in the reasons applicants give for not having made a first or second cut. When a quasi-perfect fit is sought, it's difficult for any applicant to make the match. Above all, the large number of applicants for available jobs makes success elusive. Many discovered for the first time that connections to high-profile research institutions and prominent professors matter a great deal to hiring committees. Others learned the importance of the "ability to bring funds to a hiring institution" which, in the opinion of one, "leaves green Ph.D.s out of the equation." [7] Institutional politics turned out to be more pervasive than these applicants expected. Some found faculty divided or unclear about the position offered. (In at least one instance, a candidate had to speak as a physical chemist to one interviewer and as a chemical physicist to another two doors down the hall.) Finally, the specific nature of their postdoctoral research sometimes hurt candidates in ways they didn't anticipate.

But it was the small indignities and unprofessional aspects of the job search, such as not hearing from institutions to which they had applied, not learning what disqualified them for a position, and not being told, even when they asked, whether or not they made it to the short list, that wore away applicants' confidence and fed doubts about being taken seriously. As one put it, "I felt like a baseline measuring device at some interviews. I was there for the sake of comparison only." [40] One applicant felt he had "stumbled onto the wrong search" in one in-

---

[10] Mary Ellen Hunt, formerly of Bryn Mawr College, in a personal communication to the authors.

[11] The following characterizations apply to the respondents' entire job search, not specifically to the departments through which we garnered their names.

stance, [B22] and another said he felt like a "random number among many." [B37] Or, "Interviewers don't care about me as a person and fellow human, but about how many research grants I can command." [18] Our respondents, even in this relatively small sample, encountered "token" interviews, "phony" ads [25], and departments shocked and bewildered by the number of résumés rolling in. "I was told several times that I was the only person they would have considered ten to fifteen years ago," said one of our respondents. Now, there were hundreds of potential candidates like him. [59]

Their experiences lead to the perception of absurdity, that there's no way to control this kind of "cruel roulette": "It seems [like] a game sometimes . . . [for the departments with jobs to offer] to see just how many applicants [they] can attract."[33] It is greed on the part of universities, said another, that leads them to search "for a Stephen Hawking or an Einstein" when there are many well-qualified candidates. In an ordinary job market, "I would have been a good choice," adds this respondent. [18] Part of the reason the process is so "Kafkaesque," to use one respondent's term, [B7] is that, as another explained, "it is difficult to get honest feedback." [67] The indignities magnified their disappointment and made them angry. More than a few respondents found narrow standards, insincerity, and an "us-them" mind-set among hiring faculty. "Many departments think very highly of themselves," opined one respondent, "and are more than willing to express this opinion to you, the lowly interviewee." [50]

The oversupply of candidates and poor job prospects for the near future are altering, if not obscuring, the typical career path. Left without road signs, decisions are driven less by logic, more by anxiety. Their cynicism is a sign of lost innocence. One respondent said he didn't even apply for a postdoc, "fearing the two- to three-year delay would further reduce my chances of being hired, as the market continues to deteriorate." When asked what he would have done differently with the benefit of hindsight, he said he would not have taken a postdoc because "things have only gotten worse since I graduated in 1990." [163] Admittedly, cuts have to be made when there are 200 to 500 applicants for a job, but the unwieldiness of the process has left some jobseekers with the strong sense that they will never have a fair chance at a position. Perhaps those who hire (and reject) need to reconsider the form-letter response in favor of useful feedback, lest the hiring process be perceived as even more arbitrary and capricious than it is.[12]

---

[12] Antony Starace, chair of physics at the University of Nebraska, one of the institutions which cooperated in our graduates' survey (see chap. 3), believes that chairs have become reluctant to provide specific reasons for an applicant's rejection because they fear litigation. Personal communication to the authors.

Control, autonomy, and self-sufficiency

Scientists are trained to value autonomy and the freedom to be creative. Indeed, the Ph.D. is awarded in recognition of the recipient's capacity for independent study. A struggle to launch, accelerate, or change one's career contradicts the scientist's self-image as an independent self-starter. Unemployment or underemployment is a nagging reminder that one is not fulfilling one's intellectual or career aspirations. Thus, job frustration carries a triple burden for scientists: first, the day-to-day frustration of work not sought or valued; second, fear of a future that might consist of only more of the same; and third, a personal sense of loss and embarrassment for not having become the scientist one (and one's teachers) had expected. "I am disillusioned, disenchanted, and genuinely discouraged," wrote one respondent. [7] There is "no way for my colleagues and me to remain in the field," said another. [141] "I'm unemployed," admits a respondent "which is usually taken as a 'negative' while applying." [140]

Lack of control over one's destiny turns out to be a leitmotiv in the self-reporting of young scientists. So-called technical preparation is not enough to ply the craft, at least as far as unsuccessful applicants are concerned.[13] Said one respondent:

> I've come up with a theory of enzyme catalysis (published) and
> have detailed four different experimental approaches to test it.
> This would be big news coming from someone established in
> the field, but from me, who cares? What else can I do? [137]

Thus, while control is an archetype of socialization in science education, it may be maladaptive for the times. For many, the job—the reward they so obviously deserve after so much study and accomplishment—remains out of reach.

Fitting the academic mold

In a tight job market, luck, pedigree, and an active major professor take on larger significance.[14] "It is impossible to find a job without strong inside connections," indicates one of our respondents speaking for many. [163] "It's who you know," applicants complained [41]; having a degree from a name school and the backing of some "mighty

---

[13] Mood and expectations can change radically and suddenly with the arrival of an offer. Some of our respondents, writing on institutional stationery, criticized our questionnaire for being "negative." This suggests that, although they had not competed successfully for the job at the institution which was cooperating with our survey, they did land another job somewhere else.

[14] For example, see Paula E. Stephan and Sharon G. Levin, *Shrinking the Mother Lode in Science: The Importance of Age, Place, and Time* (New York: Oxford University Press, 1992).

professor" were more important than they realized. [34] [D116] A "paper trail—publications and postdoctoral experience—are extremely important for positions that shouldn't require them," says another. [157]

Even when institutions claimed they were seeking a variety of candidates (after all, they advertised positions in widely read publications), our respondents were skeptical. Too often, they felt, cuts were made on the basis of where or with whom the applicant had studied. Had she known the "power of elitism" in this process, reported one job applicant, she "would have made sacrifices earlier" in her career to go to a "top school." [1] "Once you made it into the final ten or so for a position, [the final choice] seemed rather random," reported an applicant. [148] Indeed, job seekers in our survey often found that even their scientific achievements were secondary to a host of lesser factors such as research institution and mentor.

Quantity of publications was frequently seen by respondents as favored over quality of output (and quality of mind). "It does seem more important to have a long list of papers than high quality. . . ." [A26] But "image" was also important. "People look for very specific qualifications and too little at general abilities." [A40] One Ph.D. recipient who went into industry was considered a "quitter" by his department. Was this because the department really thought less of science in industry than academe? Or because the individual had found the job on his own? "There is extreme prejudice against anyone who doesn't fit the 'academic mold,'" another wrote. [156] "Mediocrity wins. A creative or innovative person is 'unsafe.'" [A39]

Mentoring

Potentially, the good mentor guides the new initiate; the mentor may function as advocate, buffer, provider of moral support, and placement officer. Some of our respondents were provided advice on applying and interviewing for positions by their major professors. But the majority indicated that their mentors limited their assistance to the minimum—letters of recommendation when requested by potential employers. One respondent, speaking of her postdoc adviser, said she wished she'd had someone "who would 'mentor me' (in the sense of marketing my talents to potential employers) as well as 'allow' me to work in his lab." [73] And a number of respondents agreed with the job applicant who said he wished his major professor had given him "specific advice about what to include in my vita and what to leave out, [and had shown] more willingness to call the places I was applying to and speak on my behalf." [95] Said another, "After working for [my major professor] six years, I would have hoped he would be willing to take a more active role [and make] follow-up phone calls." [A9] Other job applicants noted lack of assistance by mentors in uncovering "nontraditional alternatives." [39]

Teaching versus research

Confusion about what departments wanted was confounded by their demands for high quality teaching as well as research. Many of our respondents were angry or upset over the fact that "big 'U' departments often don't really care about teaching, and want grant-getters only." [160] Yet, the "big U's," perhaps for political reasons, would advertise teaching as a major component of available jobs. The preferences of small colleges were no easier to fathom. Some didn't care about grants, reported our respondents, only teaching. Yet several respondents expressed "surprise" at how much "high-powered research" counted, even among small colleges. Competing for a job turned out to be difficult because "second-tier institutions are looking for 'superstars' to try to get a bigger slice of a smaller [funding] pie rather than adjusting to reduced funding." [64]

Respondents were disturbed when interviewers tried to "pigeonhole" candidates, as one of our respondents put it, "as either researchers or teachers." [140] Even when academic departments claimed to favor teaching, wrote another, "there is scant . . . objective evidence sought of teaching ability." In his job search, he found hiring committees willing to hear sample lectures but not to allow him to engage in dialogue with his listeners, a vital component of his teaching repertoire. [30] Such experiences left this respondent with some doubts as to how central teaching really was to that institution. A job market that is so patently unclear about its values sends out mixed signals to young scientists, signals that make the job search even more difficult.

Lost innocence

Jobs often disappeared in midsearch owing to budget cuts, which only increased applicants' sense of being out of control. In numerous cases, the raw underbelly of science was revealed to job seekers for the first time. From one failed applicant:

> There was too much focus on who was working on the "hot topic of the week". . . [on] who was "out there" and who was "hot." I was told that if I got an offer from [another] place, that would get me an offer from my postdoc university, where they knew me quite well already. [171]

Others found themselves competing among friends, which undermines the "team model" in science: [A130]

> Colleagues and collaborators are all competitors in a fight to survive in the field. Good people are forced out and stranded. Those who remain are [set at] odds more often than working together toward common goals. [141]

Applicants soon become jaded, viewing those who hold the positions they covet as competitors:

> The fact is that a great number of those [interviewers who] tell applicants they are not qualified could not themselves get a job today. They're where they are because they were smart enough to be born 15 years earlier. [137]

Some respondents feel so uncomfortable writing about their job search that they employ the third person. In a sense, their responses reflect a role reversal, with the scientist the object of an impersonal and not fully understood experiment. The reason may be because the methodology of the department as a prospective employer is murky; the number of variables (budgets, grants, or affirmative action, for example) is unknown; and the formula for decision-making is never disclosed. Respondents resent being "lab rats" in an experiment not of their own design. It is possible that extreme reactions correlate with the reported length of search. But even those who had not been searching long respond as if they have, for the first time, glimpsed the "dark side" of their discipline and of themselves. Many have never before been rejected in an academic setting. They have been stars in their high schools and undergraduate science programs and been accepted to graduate institutions of their choice. Nothing prepared them for the harsh realities of the job search, and they have suffered severe blows to their self-esteem.

The impersonal nature of the search process is especially lamented, but how could it be otherwise? In one of the departments which mailed out our questionnaire to all declined applicants, there had been 200 candidates for the job; in another department, nearly 300 for a position. And at a third institution, two job openings in related physics fields in a single two-year period drew nearly 800 applications (some of them overlapping).[15] Not only does the impersonality of the form-letter response goad our applicants, but they suspect that it is all unfair. One told how different the treatment and tone of the interview was when he was "short listed" as against not making the initial cut.

Some of our respondents, trying to defend the profession, use "oversupply of Ph.D.s" to rationalize the difficult search process, but even they point to a lack of candor and deception on the part of colleges and universities, even hypocrisy: "Many faculty treat their work like any other nine-to-five job," writes one, "which doesn't agree with the flat-out dedication that most scientists profess." [B20] He anticipated resistance at such institutions to anyone who might possibly be a "rate

---

[15] Our survey reached only a portion of these applicants because of the two-year time frame.

buster." And when affirmative action is cited in explaining hiring practices, spurned candidates tend to conclude that quality is being compromised.

Overall, our applicants find senior faculty (1) naive; (2) prejudiced; (3) myopic: "Most chemistry faculty greatly overestimate the quality of their departments compared to departments nationwide"; [A129] and (4) overly traditional: "The meaning of success [in science] is too narrowly defined in the minds of those in charge." [143] One applicant who found a job in industry attributed his success at adapting to his new surroundings to the fact that he wasn't elitist:

> I really see the elitism of physics [more clearly] than before: departments whose job seems to be weeding out all those they think don't "make the grade" instead of working to open physics and science up . . . to those who, at first glance . . . don't "look right." In my industry work, I have been enormously helped by the fact that I am not "elitist." [152]

What does job hunting in the physical sciences teach graduates about life in science? "It's tough, it's mean, and you can never relax. The real hell starts *after* you get your Ph.D." [B31]

The Great Training Robbery[16]

Young scientists are not unaware of the current debate about the oversupply of Ph.D.s. On the Young Scientists' Network we picked up a spirited debate about proposals to cut back on Ph.D. production: *who* would go and *at what point* in their preparation? Both the American Physical Society and the American Chemical Society calculate that only 5 to 15 percent of current Ph.D. production in physics and chemistry would be curtailed if the bottom third or even the bottom half (ranked by quality) of 177 physics and 192 chemistry Ph.D. programs were eliminated. That's because the lowest-ranked have the lowest output.[17] Still, any cutbacks, the young scientists have figured out for themselves, mean fewer opportunities.

What else would be affected? The cynical among the respondents say "that nice stream of cheap graduate students and postdocs" would be diminished, as would the granting of tenure for attracting and maintaining big graduate programs. As many on the Young Scientists' Net-

---

[16] With gratitude for the title to Ivar Berg, author of *Education and Jobs: The Great Training Robbery* (Boston: Beacon Press, 1971).

[17] Forty-seven chemistry departments surveyed by *Chemical and Engineering News* in 1992, representing less than a quarter of the 192 departments that award Ph.D.s in this country, produce more than half of all the American doctoral degrees in chemistry each year.

work now perceive, Ph.D. production is entirely uncoordinated with employment opportunities for young Ph.D.s. It is linked, rather, to the continued success of older, established professors.

The Postdoctoral Position

We took advantage of the opportunity afforded by our survey to explore our respondents' perceptions of the postdoctoral experience. In some fields, the postdoc is a de facto requirement for later employment, both to season young scientists and to give them an opportunity to complete (and publish) research on their own. At its best in the past, the postdoctoral position offered an additional learning phase, comparable to a residency for a fresh M.D. The young scientist got experience in a different lab, often in a different specialty, and the combination of a "good" Ph.D. and a "good" two-year postdoc put the individual in a stronger position to do science, wherever he or she finally went to work. Without teaching, administrative, or management duties, young scientists frequently did the "best work of their careers as postdocs," recalls Robert Sproull. "Science benefited and the university benefited."[18]

In the physical sciences a postdoctoral position is typically of one to three years' duration maximum. Pay varies from field to field, but tends not to exceed $25,000 for a twelve-month work schedule. This means that these scientists, many age 30 or older, will be earning about what a B.S. chemist starts at in an industrial job.[19] This can be justified if the postdoc is truly a professional apprenticeship of limited duration. But what if it isn't? Because of their temporary nature, the quality and quantity of postdoctoral appointments have not been formally studied; nor have they even been counted in the census-taking or sampling operations.[20] Thus, our sampling, however small, is significant.

When permanent positions are scarce, the postdoc becomes a "temporary holding pattern"—in economist Alan Fechter's words—for young scientists who can't get to the next level.[21] And, in the worst of all possible cases, postdoctoral positions are extended in duration to keep

---

[18] Robert Sproull was chairman of physics and vice president for academic affairs at Cornell University prior to becoming chancellor and then president of the University of Rochester in the 1970s. The judgment quoted here is from a personal communication to the authors.

[19] That figure was $24,000 for B.S. chemists graduating between Sept. 1992 and summer 1993 based on ACS surveys reported in *Chemical and Engineering News* (Oct. 25, 1993): p. 54.

[20] Only very recently has this information gap been addressed.

[21] Alan Fechter of the National Research Council quoted in *Chemical and Engineering News* (Oct. 19, 1992): p. 40. The same is true of so-called "gypsy teachers" who work part-time at several institutions. For a description of that situation more generally than in science, see Seth Mydans, "Part-Time College Teaching Rises, as Do Worries," *The New York Times* (Jan. 4, 1995): p. B6.

down research costs. This is possible because the federal funding agencies surrender control to the local campus, which pays a bare-bones wage with no adjustments for inflation. The result is that postdoc salaries fall farther behind faculty salaries, reinforcing the second-class citizenship of the post-docs. At least one of our respondents reported having been "beaten out for a postdoc by someone with three previous appointments." [B6] And another respondent, who had spent nine years in two postdoctoral positions, found himself unable to get an academic job because his would-be employers "prefer a young, new graduate over a well-seasoned professional." [94] If graduates are in postdocs too long, everybody loses, says Fechter. In time overqualified postdocs will be seen as "damaged goods." At a startlingly young age they could be the true casualties of oversupply, stuck in "a purgatory where we wait to see if we will be admitted [through] the gates of academe." [81]

With more data available about postdocs, word has been spreading about another problem: too many people looking for postdoctoral positions. A summer 1992 ACS survey revealed a 43% postdoc acceptance rate by new Ph.D.s, up from 37% in 1991 and 34% in 1990. In 1992 placement coordinators at chemistry departments were becoming concerned with "the recent, rapid buildup of Ph.D.s accepting postdoctoral positions," as reported in *Chemical and Engineering News*.[22] In 1993 the same publication delivered a more disturbing message:

> Some new [chemistry] Ph.D.s are taking postdoctoral positions they ordinarily would not have considered and where they sometimes languish for three or four years before they find something permanent . . . . The result is a clogged pipeline.[23]

If, as some believe, about 2,000 chemists were doing postdoctoral work in 1993, this constitutes nearly a year's production of chemistry Ph.D.s. Yet, department chairs continue to report record numbers of applicants for postdocs even when there have been no advertised openings.[24]

With postdoctoral appointments scarce, respondents report averaging only one or no in-person interviews. And successful or not, appli-

---

[22] "New Graduates Face Tight Job Markets," *Chemical and Engineering News* (Oct. 19, 1992): p. 40.

[23] "New Chemistry Ph.D.s Face Sluggish Industrial, Academic Job Market," *Chemical and Engineering News* (Oct. 25, 1993): p. 44. A new "artifact" that has emerged with the poor job situation is the industrial postdoc, a temporary research position, often at a small, new company. "They're not permanent jobs, it's true, but it's that or nothing for many new graduates," says John Allison of Michigan State University, East Lansing. Some companies eventually offer permanent employment to successful postdocs.

[24] Ibid.

cants say that postdoc searches are conducted in an unprofessional manner. Many of our respondents did not expect to have to comb through advertisements for postdocs, and consider this to be an unsatisfactory way to launch a research career. Moreover, having to compete with those who are (or are perceived to be) advantaged because of race, or gender, or Ivy League connections is not what they had expected of a "scientific" search.

A wide variety of responses were received to our question, "Did the postdoc help or hinder?" Answers depended on the particular line of research that had been pursued, and to what extent the leading scientist took on the nurturing role of "second mentor." One respondent's research line turned out to be, in his words, "unsuited for easy job hunting." If he could redo his postgraduate years, he wrote, he would have redirected his research "to sexier lines." [10] Although often functioning as springboards, the postdoc experiences were also vulnerable to the subjective perceptions of hiring departments: one respondent reported that his postdoc in the national labs was viewed as second class by some of his interviewers.

Postdocs helped when they took place at prestigious institutions. One respondent who had done two sequential postdocs noted that the second had hurt because it was not at a highly regarded research university. [89] Similarly, the reputation of the adviser was important. Those with relatively unknown advisers were perturbed to discover that fact, while those with well-known advisers were candid about how important reputation is: When asked how a major professor helped in the job search, one respondent wrote, "just by being himself," explaining that this adviser's reputation was all the young scientist needed. [B42]

The overall impression with which the reader is left after perusing the responses is that, as funding tightens, the reality of the postdoctoral position is changing. What was once seen as a reservoir of enthusiastic talent is becoming a dumping ground for credentialed and capable scientists exiled from the mainstream of their discipline. The human cost of this mismatch between supply and demand must be measured in opportunities denied and careers stifled.

Rethinking Science as a Career

A key question on the Applicant Questionnaire turns out to be the one which asks our respondents why they will stay in science. Three responses emerge: Science remains the most interesting and challenging thing they can do; they are incapable of doing anything else; or they are in science because of a calculation they made early about the most productive way to employ their skills (what sociologists would term the more instrumental response). Their sense of their "calling" and their pragmatism explain respondents' willingness to keep looking for jobs during what they hope is a temporary recession.

Reactions to queries about second career choices, both in the abstract and to our specific question, "What will you do with your training if a job in science does not materialize?" revealed a wider variety of possibilities than we had anticipated, but little indication that the "second choice" would be more than just that. One applicant, who said, "I hate law," admits he will probably return to it now, after a long and fruitless job search. [83] In contrast, a space scientist whose most recent job search in science lasted a year says he is "very happy" with his computer programming position. [86] The following excerpt from a letter accompanying a questionnaire captures the essence of the pain for many of even contemplating a career switch:

> I have toyed with the idea of going to law school . . . . However, I am not sufficiently interested in the law itself. I am interested in physics, not in its application to other areas. [B17]

This applicant labored long under the impression that talent and commitment to science was all he would need to launch his career. He is now beginning to wonder whether he was wrong, and if so, what else he can do. He summarizes his circumstances eloquently.

> I hope that I have given you some impression of what life is like for people in my position—torn by the conflict between our willingness to devote ourselves entirely to our chosen profession, and our profession's unwillingness (or inability) to have us.[25] [161]

Gender Issues

Do women scientists experience the post-Ph.D. period any differently than men? A sizable number of women (47 of 268)[26] in our applicant sample from the physical sciences made it possible to separate certain questionnaire responses by gender. Gender differences appeared in answer to the question, "Why did you not apply for a particular position?" Contrary to expectations (and although we did not inquire as

---

[25] This respondent finally succeeded in finding a second postdoctoral position after sending applications to 150 institutions around the world. His only other offer in 1994 was from the Middle East. For a while, as he wrote the authors in a letter, he considered "continuing in physics on a volunteer basis or perhaps leaving the field altogether."

[26] Of 47 women (18%) in our applicant response pool, 16 women were in chemistry, 7 in astronomy, 21 in physics, 3 other. The skew in the direction of physics (atypical for the profession as a whole) had to do with the particular searches underway in the applicant pools we examined.

to marital status), male scientists[27] were just as inhibited by "spouse not thrilled by the prospect" or "not attracted to the region" as were female scientists. In addition, the average length of search for men was twice as long as for women. However, we don't know precisely what these respondents counted as "search time" (and women may be giving up sooner than men). The same interpretation problem exists regarding the higher number of interviews women get than men—either women are more desirable (hence more interviews), or they are being sought out to meet affirmative action requirements. Because of the limited number of women in the sample, we cannot draw too much from this. Even though their search time was shorter and they got more interviews, the women did not do any better (or worse) than the men.

Under pressure to hire females and minorities, certain institutions (not necessarily those who cooperated in our study) subjected individuals in our sample to unpleasant interview experiences. One female candidate was left with the perception that the institution had no intention of hiring her (or any other female) but was just going through the motions. Another wrote of her year of search, "[Mine] is still a very male-dominated field and most men have great difficulty accepting a female coworker. The students [she met during the visit] also are less willing to accept women faculty." [174] Not fitting the expected life- and work-styles were also factors. "Every woman I know who interviewed last year was questioned early in the process concerning marital status," wrote another. [151]

The impression gained from the survey and from reading mail on the Young Scientists' Network is that "us-them" dualisms abound, but for the most part, the "us" embraces all young scientists regardless of gender or race. The "thems" vary. They are sometimes the older, entrenched scientists who won't hire young scientists or retire from their jobs and make room for them; or scientists who may benefit from the tight job market which makes many more highly qualified postdocs available. In other messages, the "them" appear to be people outside science altogether, the science illiterates who don't value the contribution of science to society.

Conclusion

The applicants who responded to our questionnaire shared three major concerns. They were disenchanted by uncertainty and perceived lack of control over their future in science; they were disturbed that

---

[27] The possibilities listed were: "not interested in the position;" "not interested in the institution;" "not attracted to the region;" "knew too much about the institution;" "spouse not thrilled by the prospect;" and "not enough of an improvement."

they needed to showcase themselves after having done creditable graduate work; and they were unwilling or unable to pursue alternatives to academic employment.[28] Yet, for all their frustration with the current job scene, the young scientists we queried are remarkably constructive in thinking about how science and scientists might be better served by government, by universities, and by accrediting institutions. They recognize that so long as present conditions remain unchanged (namely, the frenzied pursuit by more and more scientists of fewer and fewer research dollars), their lives will not improve.

A case in point is the complaint by one recent Ph.D. over the reclassification of his M.S.-granting alma mater from a Research II to a Research I university. The reclassification, he tells his mates on YSN e-mail, recognizes the university's growth in research funding and doctoral production, but not the effect of that growth on the job market. "Should I be proud that [my university] is increasing its production of Ph.D.s?" he writes on the YSN. "Maybe I should try, instead, to 'enlighten' [them] on the already glutted market for Ph.D.s."

---

[28] All these concerns are also reflected on the Young Scientists' Network, where academic birth control, better and more systematic job matching systems, and information about career alternatives are frequent topics of discussion.

Reasons Given for Failed Job Applications

Question: If you have not gotten a position for which you recently applied, to what do you attribute this?

Age or Other Discriminations

I am over fifty • I'm too young • My age • Age (and experience) discrimination, since pay scale would have been higher than very fresh Ph.D. • As an older, experienced professor, I'm expensive to hire • I have too much business experience and am too old • They didn't need a woman • I may have been the target of discrimination • I was discriminated against.

Elitism (adviser or school recognition)

I did not have a big enough name on my résumé • My adviser did not have enough friends • Someone applied who was from a better school [and had] more publications.

Publications

They may have counted the number of publications only • Not enough publications • Too few publications • Not enough publications, and I'm not well known professionally • My name is not well known yet.

Size of Competition

Just too many people better than me • With so many applicants, it is always possible to find someone better • With 100-200 applicants per position, there was bound to be someone better • More than 100 applicants for one position • The fact that 60-100 people are applying for every job • The enormous number of applicants results in highly arbitrary criteria and highly specific requirements • The initial selection process was such that my credentials never received consideration • Choosing a candidate among hundreds of applicants is a complex process • Quasi-perfect fit is a requirement • Chance.

Other

My field was not "popular" • My area is in poor demand • Honesty about looking for industrial positions hurt • Tech and research in a wide variety of fields • Reluctance to hire for a third postdoc • Bias against college research • Confusion over departmental needs • Some advertised positions were never given final approval • The position would have been a step down • Too closely related to current faculty member • Better match of research interests • Departments were looking for other specialization • Incompatibility of style or personality • I was told that I lack teaching experience. • Personal factors • Negative tenure decision • Lack of specific experience with specific materials and equipment • The position required more research experience than I had • Three years experience is little compared to the people laid off from IBM and AT&T • One has to realize that there are candidates that are better suited; you also have to be lucky • I showed too little interest in the job • I missed most deadlines • I haven't completed degree • I think my cover letter was weak and possibly stressed things I shouldn't have • My proposal wasn't strong enough • Lack of ability • I did not have a postdoc and my research was not presented in a "lively" manner • The person making the decision did not carefully review the application materials • I wasn't the best applicant they could find • Departments generally want staff "button pusher" crystallographers who can churn out massive amounts of (generally) unanalyzed data.

5

Restructuring Supply, Part I

EDUCATING SCIENTISTS

It is my belief that a science degree can serve not only as a gateway to a research career, but also as a strong foundation for a variety of career paths in much the same way that a business, law, or political science degree can create many career options . . . .

—Neal F. Lane, Director, National Science Foundation[1]

T HE DEBATE about whether the U.S. needs more scientists hinges, according to many of our respondents, on what a scientist is and really does. Successful scientists can contribute to all sectors of the economy but, except for a narrow band of "switchers" among the groups we queried, this belief remains theoretical at best. "Scientists have a rigorous frame of mind useful for anything," says a scientist working in industry. "The science illiterates do not." [23][2] Workplace dynamics may be market-driven, but science-trained professionals are capable of "quick study," and ought to have many career options. [16][24][168]

These are the perceptions. The realities, however, are quite different. A former physicist in our sample in his fifties, who earned his Ph.D. in 1969 during an earlier downturn, is now a farmer. The physics training he received was "too narrow" in his view, as were the expectations of his college employer, who prohibited him from expanding his teaching of physics into social ecology. [17] An astronomer in his mid-forties who is happily employed in his profession is no less critical of

---

[1] Neal F. Lane, "Science Policy in Transition: New Opportunities" (remarks to the Council of Scientific Society Presidents, May, 1994).

[2] Numbers in brackets refer to the specific questionnaires from which direct quotations have been taken. To retain anonymity, the authors sequentially numbered questionnaires upon arrival. Numbers preceded by "E" refer to an e-mail questionnaire distributed and responded to on the Young Scientists' Network. Questionnaires and responses were later archived.

academe. He writes that scientists as well as their employers need to "broaden their perspectives" because "there is too much emphasis on academic careers and too [little training] for the more versatile careers that the nation probably needs." [24]

What kinds of "more versatile" careers might scientists aim for? It is one thing to speculate about the "emerging occupations" that Congressman George Brown sometimes refers to, or to wonder who will do the "other tasks of science" sketched by Linda Wilson (see page 38).[3] It is quite another to count on them. Responsible academics are understandably reluctant to train scientists for positions not yet fully defined. Yet, in our view, that is exactly what must be done. Once new kinds of scientists are trained, their availability may well create new kinds of jobs (a reversal of the usual dynamic where demand generates supply). The reason? With multiple skills in hand and different expectations about what a scientist can contribute, the next generation of professionals would surely prove their worth to a wider variety of employers. True, the first round might be difficult (physicists in regulatory agencies, chemists in the insurance industry), but these versatile professionals could lead the way in creating new jobs for others like themselves.

One reason there seems to be so few options for scientists outside of science is that professionals tend to hire people like themselves. This may be why science-trained professionals are not recruited as enthusiastically as lawyers and M.B.A.s to government and industry in the U.S. as they are in Japan, for example, where a critical mass of midlevel managers hold degrees in science and engineering.

Science as a First Career

Although some of the nation's best scientists have used science as a "launching pad," they don't think about their careers in this way. After a decade or more of productive research, these men and women find themselves plying a consulting or management career, running large laboratories and centers, authoring textbooks or, even more distant from the bench, administering large university or industrial departments and heading up nonprofit organizations. Some of them say that they are no longer physicists, chemists, geologists, or astronomers—that is, no longer scientists—once they have made such moves. Returning from a three-year stint at the Advanced Research Projects Agency of the Department of Defense to a university position as vice president for academic affairs, Robert Sproull would routinely correct one of the au-

---

[3] George Brown uses the term when he speaks informally. For his more formal rendering of the argument, see George E. Brown, Jr., "New Ways of Looking at U.S. Science and Technology," *Physics Today* (Sept. 1994): pp. 3 ff.

thors whenever she introduced him as a physicist. "I am no longer a physicist," he would say. "I am no longer practicing physics."

Other successful advocates for science (like Radford Byerly, a physicist who worked on Congressman George Brown's Space, Science and Technology Committee in the House and is a consultant to the National Research Council) admit that, had they known in advance how they would be using their science and so informed their graduate school advisers, they might never have gotten Ph.D.s (might not even have been accepted to graduate school). What a graduate professor was looking for then (and now), thinks Byerly, was a Ph.D. student who would extend and enhance the professor's own research career.[4] In view of this parochialism, is it any wonder one of our respondents never felt comfortable telling her graduate committee that she longed to leave physics for a research career in biology? [91] How much harder it would have been to leave physics for precollege teaching or for science journalism, or to become a science attaché to one of our embassies.

Commercially-Oriented Scientific Skills

The idea of developing in some portion of the nation's young people "commercially-oriented scientific skills" is a desirable alternative to "academic birth control," writes Francis Slakey in *The Chronicle of Higher Education*. Slakey, a science-policy administrator for the American Physical Society, suggests that instead of trying to remake universities into "high-speed economic engines," the administration and Congress should encourage them to produce "high-octane economic fuel"— namely, a work force with commercially relevant scientific skills.[5]

> The bachelor of science and master of science degrees in the physical sciences should prepare students to move smoothly into industrial, commercial, or even entrepreneurial activities, instead of just preparing them for further academic study. Our nation's high-tech industries are looking for technically trained employees, and undergraduates in the physical sciences could be contenders. But in many universities, the B.S. is just a one-way ticket to graduate "schoolville." And a master's is like getting an "incomplete" on a report card.[6]

Slakey wants a restructuring of the supply of science-trained professionals, but is it reasonable to expect that current faculty and administrators will promote these new science degrees? One way to think about

---

[4] Radford Byerly, personal communication to the authors.

[5] Francis Slakey, "Point of View," *The Chronicle of Higher Education* (Jan. 19, 1994): p. A52.

[6] Ibid.

these issues is in terms of niche-filling, or stratifying institutions by function. But this is not part of our tradition. The university system enjoys federal support without federal planning. The question to which we shall return in chapter 7 is whether the federal government ought to take responsibility for assigning institutional priorities and for filling particular niches.[7]

In past years, there were only a few career paths for holders of science degrees, whether B.S., M.S., or Ph.D. A set of early career decisions governed the extent of a student's training and tended to foreclose other options. Young people who were not as enthusiastic about research as about applications of science found themselves directed toward engineering, and anyone who was ambivalent about the single-minded devotion required of a science graduate chose another field. Today, as Neal Lane, Linda Wilson, and John Armstrong (see page 85) suggest, there are many more scientific tasks to be accomplished by more versatile professionals. But so long as the traditional career paths do not include these new options, cutbacks in research support by government and private companies must lead to cutbacks in recruitment and training of future scientists.

What Kind of Training?

As we have seen in their responses to our questionnaires, the analytic rigor and challenge of their Ph.D. training seems to have had lasting value for the older survey respondents. When asked, "What skills derived from your scientific training have proved most valuable throughout your career?" we received answers such as the following: "logical approach to problem solving"; [67] "thinking critically"; [79] "analytic and deductive reasoning"; [C6] "the ability to work with complex instrumentation"; [66] and "assembling knowledge." [163] One said—perhaps tongue-in-cheek—that science was as good a preparation for a career in marketing as any other. "I can easily understand the theory of anything I am involved in since it is simple compared to physics," the respondent commented. [164] Another, who stayed in science, attributed his analytical skills directly to his training: "When I'm right, I know I'm right. And I am always aware when I am not." [65]

Few of our older respondents—even those who were no longer "doing science" professionally—found fault with the hands-on aspects of science that took up so much of their training. On the contrary, one commented that what industry needs are "fewer managers and more

---

[7] Stratification (or specialization) has been achieved in certain fields at certain institutions. For most of the recent past, only two universities, the University of Arizona and University of Rochester, have offered the Ph.D. in optical sciences. As a result of this specialization, the two programs have had little difficulty, at least so far, in placing their students.

'doers.'" [C2] Those trained in science can contribute to technically-oriented enterprises (especially product development) better, they felt, than those trained only in business or management. It was in chemistry and mathematics that a chemist, responding to our query, says she learned to "separate material that was essential from [that which was not], and to organize work assignments . . . logically and clearly."[8] [M32]

Younger Scientists' Views

Opinions like these may be more common among established scientists. To reach a younger cohort sensitive to the discrepancies between what they were trained to do in science and what they found themselves having to do, we returned to the Young Scientists' Network in the summer of 1994 and put these questions to any who would respond: (1) Had you known what the job situation would be, what would you have done differently in your graduate study? (2) What courses, apprenticeships, or training would have added value to your degree? (3) What nonscience electives are you finding of value in your current job? (4) Does your strategy for what to do next include seeking another degree? If so, which degree and field? Why will you seek another degree?[9]

In response to the first question, many of our respondents would have repeated their previous course of study, but almost as many would have sought M.B.A., computer science, or M.D. degrees instead. One 1994 Ph.D. in physics would have changed from pure to applied science, such as surface physics or high tech superconductor devices. For those who would have pursued science "no matter what," courses in "C" programming language and the Unix operating system would have (they think) boosted their marketability.[10] Others would have benefited, they think, from courses in business, political science ("because science has become so political," one wrote), architectural drawing, pharmacology, statistics ("with an eye to process control"), medical imaging, and microwave circuit design. An additional master's degree in engineering tempted some, but others think only a few courses and not a degree in engineering would "help people trying to go into industry." [E14] Courses in education or education administration would

---

[8] Of the science education skills mentioned by one chemist as not very useful or adaptable was "memorizing large amounts of data for exams." [M6]

[9] All direct quotations are taken from the YSN response to authors' inquiry.

[10] Brian Schwartz, professor of physics in the CUNY system and outgoing education chair of the American Physical Society, knows well how important these programming languages are in the "real world," in contrast to Fortran, the programming language of science in the academy (see p. 36). He has arranged with the Baruch School of Business in the CUNY system to have all his Ph.D. students learn at least "C" before graduating. Personal communication to the authors.

aid in getting into academe. Additional work in applied math was also recommended as an aid to science students not sure of their direction, and shop courses would also add value: "If you can make it yourself, you save a lot of overhead." [E25] Some respondents complained of a lack of training in grant-writing. The attitude of their professors had seemed to be that when students left, they would know just how to do it.

A question on helpful courses outside a science major brought forth a new metaphor on an e-mail response: "Knowledge should be a 'cratered landscape'—in-depth but over a scattered range of topics—as opposed to too narrow specialization." [E23] A scientist who works in defense and technology policy wrote that "a summer internship program in another lab, or even an internship doing something totally different, i.e., nonscience," would have been helpful. "Essentially, [I should have] used the time in grad school to continue to broaden my knowledge base, [to] gain breadth as well as depth." [E38]

Many young scientists bemoaned the fact that they had not worked summers in a nonacademic environment. Several of our respondents thought a co-op term in industry would have enhanced their degrees. A younger survey participant who had just started a Ph.D. in physics and had not yet chosen a subfield also felt "more apprenticeships or summer positions would [help] greatly both to give me a better idea about particular subfields in physics and chances to talk with people in those fields." [E46] One respondent thought he would have benefited from a year abroad for the opportunity to master at least one foreign language.

There is reason to ask whether extra training and skills might be achieved more efficiently, and whether the structure of most graduate and undergraduate programs in physical science continues to be appropriate for changing times. As one respondent wrote, "A second degree would delay my entrance into the job market until retirement age," [E45] and wondered why "we can't confer what needs to be learned with the first degree." Several agreed with the respondent who said of "further study or degrees":

> I feel that I [already] have plenty of training and skills. What is necessary is not to get credentialed in another field, but to convince employers in the numerous areas where I can apply [those] skills . . . that I am worth hiring and am probably able to do a much better job than the bachelor's degree holders that they are currently hiring . . . [E50]

There is always some discussion about redesigning the Ph.D. in the physical sciences, about alternative degrees in interdisciplinary areas (materials science, chemical biology), and about programs leading to general doctor of science degrees. Historically, alternate degrees have not attracted many sponsors or enrollees. Is now the time to revive those discussions? Are we ready to critically reassess undergraduate and graduate programs in science?

Revisiting the Ph.D.

In a talk given at the University of Virginia in March 1994, John Armstrong, retired IBM vice president for science and technology and visiting professor of electrical engineering and computer science, asked provocatively, "What is a Science or Engineering Ph.D. For?"[11] He began by describing Ph.D. training in the sciences as an apprenticeship, noting that graduate students bond early and tightly to individual professors. The attachment, he said, is so intense that apprentices will identify more strongly with their professor's research group than with the department or the university from which they will get their degree. Although qualification by standardized testing or certification (common abroad) would be an alternative, Armstrong is not ready to go that far. Instead, he recommends an "enhanced apprenticeship" to counter Ph.D. training methods that are "too narrow intellectually, too campus-centered, and too long."[12]

In fact, said Armstrong, students at the Ph.D. level in physical science are more broadly educated than they realize. This difference between perceptions and realities leads to what he called in his talk "the Ph.D. paradox": "One thinks one has mastered a very narrow field; in fact, one has been trained as an advanced technical generalist."[13] The tragedy is that most of the Ph.D.s do not value this capability because their professors seldom do either. Armstrong would change this by requiring "scientific and technical breadth in the graduate curriculum," as well as "time spent off campus in a setting where technical knowledge is actually used."[14] Armstrong suggests that students have a minor as well as a major.

Even more urgent is that graduate professors rethink the relative weight given to research results as against research training. Leo Kadanoff, a physicist at the University of Chicago, wants to require faculty applicants for federal grants to list what has become of their former students.[15] Armstrong agrees. "For the next decade or so, the training in many fields will be more important than the research results," he says.[16] This may be, but so long as graduate students and post-

---

[11] John A. Armstrong, "What is a Science or Engineering Ph.D. For?" Mar. 9, 1994. Originally given as the third of Armstrong's Karl T. Compton lectures at MIT on Nov. 10, 1993, abridged as "Rethinking the Ph.D." in *Issues in Science and Technology* 9, no. 4 (1994): p. 19.

[12, 13, 14] Ibid.

[15] Leo P. Kadanoff, "Greats," *Physics Today* (Apr. 1994): p. 9. See chap. 7 for more on this.

[16] John A. Armstrong, personal communication to the authors.

docs are evaluated on number of publications, there will be pressure to publish at the expense of developing breadth. A desirable change would be for graduates to include in their résumés alternate experience and added skills outside areas of specialization—and, of course, for future employers to weigh these favorably. Graduate training, most authorities now agree, should aim to enlarge the repertoire of students' skills. But how is this to come about if the value system is not changed as well?

Marvin Goldberger, dean of science and professor of physics at the University of California, San Diego and former chancellor of Caltech, also calls for shortening and broadening the Ph.D., above all reducing its "slave labor" aspect. He sits on a National Academy of Sciences panel that has questioned traditional measures used to evaluate Ph.D. programs. One new measure the panel is considering is how well a particular Ph.D. program "broadens students' interests and capabilities."[17] Privately, many professors are proud when their students use their science in industrial management, government service, or as teachers and professors in nonresearch institutions. But publicly, such choices are still thought to be nonstandard.

Armstrong and Goldberger are physicists. But a leading chemistry educator comes to many of the same conclusions about his field. Truman Schwartz, writing for *The Journal of Chemical Education,* characterizes graduate chemistry programs as "successful at producing Ph.D.s who know more and more about less and less."[18] The consequences of this "tyranny of overspecialization" are, first, that it is difficult for a liberal arts college (like his own) to hire a physical chemist who, for example, "has taken a single [graduate] course in organic or inorganic chemistry, or an analytical chemist who has ventured into physical chemistry—to say nothing of physics or mathematics."

> The required graduate minor has apparently gone the way of
> the language requirement. And the greater the reputation of
> the Ph.D.-granting institution, the smaller the quantity of for-
> mal course work that seems to be expected for the degree.[19]

The problem, Schwartz believes, is that graduate programs in chemistry are requiring fewer and fewer courses, and that some institutions have eliminated comprehensive and even cumulative examinations. In

---

[17] Marvin Goldberger, personal communication to the authors.

[18] Truman Schwartz, "Graduate Education in Chemistry: More and More about Less and Less," *Journal of Chemical Education* 71 (Aug. 1994): pp. 949-950.

[19] Ibid.

place of breadth, Schwartz writes, graduate students "are expected to join a research group some time during their first semester." A result, aside from poorer graduate education, is that "individual faculty members become recruiters for their own research groups and only incidentally for the university."[20]

Schwartz grants that a small number of truly gifted and dedicated students need a minimum of formal instruction. But the majority of graduate students can profit from structured education as well as from the apprenticeship of a research laboratory. Furthermore, early and excessive specialization runs the risk of excluding just those underrepresented individuals that the faculty should be attracting to careers in chemistry. "Many of these students," Schwartz comments, "are underprepared—academically, personally, or socially—to enter a research group immediately on receipt of a B.A. or B.S. And a sink-or-swim environment is hardly nurturing."[21] But even for those B.S. or B.A. graduates who are prepared for research, graduate education is lagging behind a changing profession.

> Some of the most interesting problems are at the interfaces between chemistry and biology, physics, engineering, geology, and other disciplines. In fact, these interfaces are fast disappearing. The discrete disciplinary spectrum of midcentury has become a continuum, and the future is bound to become even more interdisciplinary . . . . The complex challenges of interdisciplinary research demand a broader, more thorough preparation than does a more traditional disciplinary focus."[22]

Truman Schwartz, John Armstrong, and Marvin Goldberger are powerful voices for change, but where are the new graduate education models to come from? And what will cause university reward and funding structures to become receptive to them?

An excellent start is being made by the American Chemical Society with its "special presidential task force on doctoral education" chaired by chemist David K. Lavallee of City University of New York. The task force has two objectives: to reduce the total number of Ph.D.-granting departments and ensure the high quality of those that remain (the stratification or niche-filling strategy referred to earlier); and secondly— and even more pertinent here—to "develop more broadly trained and

---

[20] Ibid.

[21] Truman Schwartz, personal letter to the authors.

[22] Ibid. Schwartz refers his readers to Mary Good, *Biotechnology and Materials Science: Chemistry for the Future* (Washington, D. C.: American Chemical Society, 1988).

adaptable scientists and engineers to function in the multidisciplinary, rapidly changing environment of the chemical research enterprise."[23]

In April 1994 the ACS task force presented a preliminary report which included recommendations similar to many of Schwartz's proposals— that graduate programs provide a broader exposure to chemistry and related subjects and that graduate minors in biology, physics, geology, and computer science play a larger role in graduate education in chemistry. The task force also recommended (echoing John Armstrong) additional personnel exchanges between academe and industry, arguing that "graduates are too often 'clones' of their professors and are not being trained with the team building and entrepreneurial skills required for success in today's industrial world."[24] But most impressive was the willingness of the task force to tackle federal funding issues head-on.

As a first step, the preliminary ACS report calls for more graduate fellowships to go directly to students in order to disassociate graduate student support from faculty research grants. Although this change would reduce the size of faculty research funding on a project-by-project basis, the task force claims it would not alter support of faculty overall (though it might alter university power relationships). Another option would be to award graduate traineeships or fellowships which delegate authority (and accountability) for support of students to departments in block-grant style. Harry Wasserman, professor emeritus of organic chemistry at Yale University and on the board of the Dreyfus Foundation, says the Ph.D. in science, unlike other fields, is so much a "collaborative relation between a mentor's scholarly work and a student's, [that] the student always has to have a funded professor and the professor always has to have students." Although he—and the ACS task force—have yet to endorse departmental fellowships, they are seen as possible alternatives.[25] Alan Fechter, former staff director of the National Research Council's Office of Scientific and Engineering Personnel, wants to go further.

> Even when Ph.D. programs . . . are improved, there should always be different programs for different kinds of people. Graduate education should not produce a homogeneous commodity, but provide an opportunity for people to move to another part of the program as they see their career interests change and their capabilities develop.[26]

---

[23] David Lavallee, personal communication to the authors.

[24] ACS Preliminary Report, *Shaping the Future: The Chemical Research Environment in the Next Century*, Apr. 1994, p.16.

[25] Harry Wasserman, personal communication to the authors.

[26] Alan Fechter, personal communication to the authors.

The Alternatives

One altogether new graduate program, specifically designed for industrial chemists, is the "doctor of chemistry" (D.Chem.) degree offered by the University of Texas at Dallas since 1983. Trying to be the science equivalent of a doctor of medicine degree, the program is designed to train problem-solvers, "clinicians" who apply knowledge, rather than researchers who extend knowledge. Course work for the D.Chem. provides more breadth than that required for the typical Ph.D. because candidates do not have to specialize in organic, physical, analytical, or other branches of chemistry. What's really different is the replacement of a Ph.D. dissertation with three year-long practicums, of which only the third involves an original research paper (the first is an apprenticeship, the second requires the student to work full time as a professional in an industrial or governmental R&D laboratory).[27] So far, seventeen students have availed themselves of the D.Chem., and all hold good research positions in industry. But it has been difficult to sell the program both to candidates and to other institutions. Only thirty-five are currently enrolled, and a sister program at the University of Texas at Arlington, modeled on that at Dallas, is being eliminated. In the nearly twelve years since the program was founded, apart from U.T. Arlington's, no others have appeared—a fact which ought to give new Ph.D. program designers pause.

At the University of Maryland at College Park, Robert Yuan, professor of microbiology, intends to combine the Ph.D. in molecular biology (including dissertation) with a master's of science in technology management. Maryland is especially well suited to this promising idea because it has long housed a successful technology management master's program in biotechnology which offers a common core of management courses from which students can branch into technical areas like biotechnology, information-aided engineering, and environmental applications. The rationale for the new degree, Yuan writes, is the following:

> Fifty percent of all Ph.D.s in the life sciences are no longer working at the bench five to ten years after they receive their degrees . . . . They are in industry, government, consulting, and teaching. And nothing in the training we provide prepares them for those activities.[28]

---

[27] See a published description of the program by Lynn A. Melton, "The Doctor of Chemistry Program," *Journal of Chemical Education* 68 (Feb. 1991): pp. 142-144. Updated information courtesy of Duane Hrncir, Department of Chemistry, University of Texas at Dallas, in a personal communication to the authors.

[28] Robert Yuan, personal communication to the authors.

The problem, Yuan says, is even more acute abroad, where there is a lesser tradition of management science. Only the *grands écoles*, the French upper schools for management and administration, offer anything like training in the management of science. But there, he explains, the science taught is all conceptual and not research oriented.

The plan is to fuse the Ph.D. and M.Sc. programs at Maryland which will allow students to complete both in six years. "Fuse" is an appropriate word because the combination will not simply be an add-on. As Yuan and his colleagues envision it, the basic course work for the Ph.D. is to be a platform from which students can select three career tracks: research, teaching, or management and administration. The Ph.D. course work will also be nontraditional. A case-study approach is planned. For the teaching track, teacher training seminars will be linked to TA experiences in undergraduate courses. For the management and administration track, an active research program will be studied in detail, first as a way of understanding the science involved. Then before leaving the topic, students will engage in a discussion of the kind of questions technical managers would be facing, such as how a researcher would get funding to continue this line of inquiry, or how the research might eventually be commercialized.

Conclusion

Redesigning the Ph.D. degree in science is something many educators appear to be talking about, but there is not much action to report. While we did not go looking for new types of Ph.D. programs in researching this chapter (we were content to lay out the criticisms and the argument), what we found were ad hoc adjustments of old doctoral programs. How can these be expanded, and what is necessary for them to be taken seriously?

One physicist turned survey researcher is offering some needed feedback to graduate departments in the physical sciences. To document the educational needs of today's science professionals, Steven Smith has initiated a "Ph.D. employment and career survey" to be sent (as soon as funding is secured) to Ph.D. graduates in physics, astronomy, and chemistry. Of the fourteen work-activity codes Smith has created for respondents to choose from, only one is in "basic research."[29] The rest represent related careers. The list is not meant to be exhaustive, but is an indication that Smith, at least, is willing to count certain ancillary occupations as legitimate for Ph.D. scientists. Now, to persuade the professoriate of these realities, and of their obligation to further the ambitions of students who don't want—or realistically can't expect—to pursue an academic career.

---

[29] The rest range from "accounting" and "report and technical writing and editing" to "design of equipment." The "Ph.D. Employment and Career Survey," a proposal by Steven Smith to the American Physical Society, was shared with the authors in draft form.

6

Restructuring Supply, Part II

REINVENTING THE MASTER'S DEGREE AND REVITALIZING UNDERGRADUATE PROGRAMS

I F, AS MANY critics are beginning to think, the Ph.D. degree—or even certain variants of it—is not going to be the best terminal degree for all science-trained professionals, then what degree do we recommend? There are some European models, the "license doctorate" and the so-called "doctor of science," which train scientists to run sophisticated laboratories, albeit not to create new knowledge. Some say these are not true doctorates but the equivalents of master's degrees. While this may be true in terms of years expended and technical content, the European degrees are valued highly. In our system, the master's degree in physical science tends to be perceived as a stepping stone, a consolation prize, or, as Francis Slakey puts it (see page 81), an "incomplete."[1]

Is it any wonder, then, that of all the master's degrees awarded in the U.S. in one recent year, a mere 1.9% (5,737 of a total 309,762) were given in all the physical sciences combined, compared to 23% in management and business and 26% in education? These figures come from a 1993 study of master's education in the U.S., commissioned by the Council of Graduate Schools and supported by the Pew Trust.[2] Authors Conrad, Haworth, and Millar, echoing Slakey, note that in many fields the master's degree is not seen as a separate degree, but as a "postbaccalaureate" or "predoctoral" certificate. Yet, in business, education, engineering, nursing, and in some emerging fields such as microbiology and environmental studies, study for a master's degree is

---

[1] Francis Slakey, "Point of View," *The Chronicle of Higher Education* (Jan. 19, 1994): p.A52.

[2] Clifton F. Conrad, Jennifer Grant Haworth, and Susan Bolyard Millar, *A Silent Success: Master's Education in the United States* (Baltimore: The Johns Hopkins University Press, 1993), pp. 19-20.

coming to be viewed as "an important means for enriching the knowledge base and skills of preprofessionals in an information-centered society."[3] Indeed, say the authors, people with master's education constitute the professionals upon which business, industry, education, government, and the nation's health care systems are increasingly coming to depend for "expertise and leadership."[4]

What kind of *professional* master's degrees might we invent for science?[5] And how, once these degrees are in place, could they be marketed to faculty, students, and to the employing and subsidy-paying public? If one looks to the master's degree more generally, one finds that instead of training producers of scholarship, the traditional purpose of graduate education, master's educators aim to produce people who are able to use the products of scholarship in their work and who are familiar with "the practical aspects of emerging problem areas."[6]

Except for the physical sciences then, master's education in the U.S. is on a high growth curve, both in terms of number of degrees awarded (309,762 in 1989-90, compared to 208,291 in 1969-70, an increase of 48%) and number of programs. Whereas 621 colleges and universities granted master's degrees in 1961, almost twice as many (1,192) did so in 1985.[7] Many of the new master's programs are in interdisciplinary and emerging fields such as environmental studies, urban problems, health care for the aged, and genetic counseling. But several represent efforts by faculty in the humanities and social sciences to supply a more useful education for their liberal arts graduates. Among these new fields, housed in the traditional disciplines, are applied anthropology, applied or "public" history, bioethics, public policy (sometimes with science or technology subfield options), and applied philosophy.[8]

Although few professional master's degrees are earned in the physical sciences, we find professional master's degrees in science subsumed under two rubrics, "career advancement programs" and "apprenticeship programs" (which include engineering and microbiology). Faculty who direct these look both ways, so to speak, in everything they do. One direction is to the need of their master's candidates to become "practitioner-experts" in the nonuniversity workplace, so that wherev-

---

[3] Ibid., p.xiii.

[4] Ibid., p. xiv.

[5] The term "professional master's" is used here to avoid the uncomplimentary but more common nomenclature, "terminal master's."

[6] Donald Spencer, "The Master's Degree in Transition," *Communicator* (1986), quoted in Conrad et. al., *A Silent Success*, p. 17.

[7] All data in this paragraph are from studies undertaken in 1987 and 1983 (respectively) by Jules LaPidus, Nancy Nash, and Elizabeth Hawthorne, quoted in Conrad et. al., *A Silent Success*, p. 18.

[8] Quoting Donald Spencer, Conrad et. al., *A Silent Success*, p. 17.

er they go, they will be respected.[9] The other is toward the needs of business and industry. In addition to helping students network and inviting recruiters to campus, faculty members prepare them for professional interviews.[10] As a result, apart from a high level of technical proficiency and scientific acumen, students in career advancement and apprenticeship programs develop self-confidence, a professional identity, and what the authors call "a changed perspective." This comes from the faculty's own changed perspective: they see themselves not as repositories of knowledge but as coaches, providing constant feedback to their students.[11]

An employer, associated with a master's program in microbiology studied by Conrad, Haworth, and Millar, confirms this. Graduates of the program, he told the evaluators, "know how to face the frustrations of research, how to work through problems, how to get things done." Another goal expressly aimed for and achieved in the master's level microbiology program is scientific maturity, defined as "learning how to think scientifically [and being] able to design experiments."[12]

In some cases, the master's degree turns out not to be a terminal degree at all. Master's students frequently decide to go on to study for the Ph.D. either because they become "enamored"—as one student reported—with the subject, or because they find a new discipline (or interdiscipline) with interesting possibilities.[13] By the time they near completion of their master's degrees, their interest in the degree as a credential has been largely replaced by a new appreciation for their field and a new understanding of what occupational roles they might fill.

Master's Degrees in Science

Can some of today's graduate students be directed toward new and respected master's programs in science? David K. Lavallee (of the previously mentioned ACS presidential task force on graduate education in chemistry) would welcome "appropriate" master's programs, so long as they had a defined purpose, for example, "analytical methods in environmental chemistry."[14] As he sees it, the master's degree would work in fields in which (1), it takes more than a bachelor's degree to become proficient; (2), additional training is better done on the job than in the

---

[9] Conrad et. al., *A Silent Success*, p. 68.

[10] Ibid., p. 233.

[11] Ibid.

[12] Conrad et al., *A Silent Success*, pp. 239-240.

[13] Ibid., p. 239.

[14] David K. Lavallee, personal communication to the authors.

university; or (3), there is a local industrial demand for certain specialists. NSF Director Neal Lane has also talked favorably about professional master's programs as reported in *Physics Today*.[15] Why, then, are there so few takers? Werner Wolf, chairman of the department of applied physics at Yale University, gives us one answer:

> The courses that master's students are required to take . . . are generally the same as those taken by regular Ph.D. students, which tend to be quite theoretical and geared to advanced research rather than to broadening the student's general training. Thus, a student who stops his or her studies at [the master's level] is likely to be regarded as a basic researcher who didn't make it.[16]

Wolf says universities can avoid this problem by offering practical courses emphasizing use of instrumentation, and by educating potential employers as to the strengths of the graduates of these programs. Such contacts with industry, he believes, will in time become "self-sustaining," so long as university faculty are responsive to feedback from employers and from students alike.

Indeed, it is the lack of information about the potential market for master's students in science, particularly among the "best" Ph.D. departments, that is keeping M.S. programs from multiplying, according to John Armstrong.[17] Perhaps there is also fear that professional master's programs will attract science students who would have pursued the Ph.D., or even that M.S.s might take jobs from Ph.D.s. To get at some of these issues and to find out what kinds of professional master's degree programs are currently being offered in the physical sciences, the authors did a telephone survey during the fall of 1994. Following is the result of those phone interviews with program directors or department chairs. Our purpose was to find out not only about the nature of their existing programs, but to ask about plans for the future.[18]

Some Examples

Miami University, Oxford, Ohio, offers both M.A. and M.S. degrees in physics in a program that originated in the 1930s. In the mid-1980s the faculty added a research thesis requirement to the M.S. degree to

---

[15] "Reinventing the Future," physics roundtable, *Physics Today* (Mar. 1994): p. 30.

[16] Werner P. Wolf, "Is Physics Education Adapting to a Changing World?" *Physics Today* (Oct. 1994): p. 55.

[17] John Armstrong, personal communication to the authors.

[18] This round of interviews was largely conducted by Jacqueline Raphael, chief research and editorial assistant for this book. See "About the Authors," p. 145.

distinguish it from the M.A. Typically, fifteen to nineteen students are enrolled per year, of whom one to four are women and two to four are foreign nationals. Unlike many graduate programs in physics around the country, foreign students are in the minority.

Paul Scholten, director of graduate programs, says students choose Miami's M.S. in physics program for several reasons. Unsure of whether they should go on for a Ph.D., some are looking for a trial experience at the master's level. Others, whom Scholten describes as having "caught fire" late in their undergraduate careers, are looking for more physics and better marks in physics courses in order to get into Ph.D. programs elsewhere. Some master's candidates are working teachers who would rather do a master's degree in physics than one in education, and still others want nonacademic careers in industry or government. Their course work consists primarily of advanced physics, but options in education, for example, are allowed. Some master's candidates will do their thesis in an experimental laboratory, others in computational theory. Not surprisingly, given their different motivations for choosing the program, fully half of Miami's physics master's students go into private industry or government; the other half continue in graduate programs, usually physics or electrical engineering.

Scholten and his colleagues recommend that master's students take advantage of courses outside physics, such as one in technical writing offered by the English department, or one in entrepreneurship in the school of business. Since, as Scholten sees it, more and more master's degree candidates will be heading into private industry (especially to small entrepreneurial businesses), courses in business and technical and scientific communication will make graduates more versatile and more desirable.

Northern Arizona University's physics department currently offers only a master's in science teaching, but is considering a new, more industry-oriented postbaccalaureate degree program. According to chairman Barry Lutz, one goal would be to meet the needs of semiconductor manufacturers such as Intel and Motorola for workers trained in solid-state surface physics. (Lutz says his department has inquired as to the kinds of technical people these industries are hiring, and "they're not looking for research physicists.") The department's other objective would be to give graduates from liberal arts astronomy programs the advanced physics background they sometimes lack in order to pursue graduate work in astronomy and astrophysics.

Lutz is not confident that Ph.D. astronomers and astrophysicists will find jobs. But he sees NAU's proposed program as preparing good physics students, who haven't been turned off by the job crunch, for "other types of science careers," while retaining the option of trying their luck in research science. Those alternative careers could begin immediately or in future years. His aim is to give graduates long-term flexibility. Although the program will be small (Lutz is considering ten students at the outset), he hopes his graduates' immediate employability will convince others to advocate similar kinds of change. The curriculum is not set, but one thing is sure: students heading off to industry will be required to do a research project of significance to industry.

California State University, Fresno: The professional master's program in chemistry at California State University, Fresno demonstrates David K. Lavallee's contention (page 93) that a master's program can succeed when there is specialized regional employment. Fresno is located in one of the nation's richest agricultural areas, and career opportunities in the region are in the environmental and food processing industries. Of special interest to the university are those companies with analytical laboratories. Graduate students in the professional chemistry master's program often find employment in the region's industrial labs while they are still in school. Seven of the current twenty, reports director Ron Marhenke, are employed at least part time in an analytical laboratory or on an agriculture-related project on campus. Another reason for the program's appeal is that, under the California Master Plan, the state universities may offer a joint Ph.D. only with the University of California. Thus, students who want to stay in the area have fewer options for graduate school.

Although Fresno's M.S. program requires chemistry courses in at least four of five areas (analytical, biochemistry, inorganic, organic, and physical), students specialize when they choose their thesis project. Most students do projects in analytical chemistry due to faculty members' ties to local industry. These projects typically deal with locally grown products such as fruit juices and wines, problems of local industry such as groundwater issues, toxins in wastewater, sulfur dioxide residues in table grapes, and pesticide residues in air, or improvements in the typing of blood residues. The work is often done in conjunction with agriculture M.S. candidates at Fresno who can concentrate in agricultural chemistry.

Still, industry-bound students form the largest contingent in the program. Of the enrollees preparing to go on for Ph.D.s, many are international students who wish to test their ability in an English-language program involving modern research and instrumentation. A few simply want to improve their academic record. The smallest group, still a significant number, are those preparing to pursue careers in medical or pharmaceutical fields. The program, says Marhenke, is not designed primarily for the health professions, but such students do benefit from it, especially those in biochemistry. So far, the high nonresident tuition has deterred out-of-state applicants. As a result, one-third of the enrollment is international, one-third Cal State Fresno graduates, and one-third other Californians. It should take only two years to complete the M.S. in chemistry, but three years is probably average, six years for those working full time. The department is considering changes that would make its nonthesis master's degree option more available to students who have full-time jobs.

Master's in Business for Scientists

Modifying existing master's of business programs to attract and better serve science students is another strategy to make science graduates more flexible. Two examples, Temple University's master's of business with chemistry concentration, and Cornell University's plan for enrolling scientists and science-trained professionals in its Johnson School of Management, illustrate somewhat different curricula and goals. A third example, from Pennsylvania State University, is an accelerated bachelor's of science with master's of business sequence that students can complete in five years.

Five years ago Temple University's chemistry department cooperated with its school of business to design a concentration within the M.B.A. program to prepare B.A. or B.S. graduates in chemistry with a "competitive edge in management."[19] Philadelphia and its environs host a number of important chemical companies, and conversations with these firms suggested that a chemistry M.B.A. would fill a niche. The program includes all the usual M.B.A. requirements—accounting, economics, management, finance, computer and information systems, human resources, and marketing—with a difference: students may concentrate in chemistry. Students do not necessarily have to have majored in the subject to be admitted, but they do have to have taken courses that will prepare them for graduate-level work in advanced instrumental methods, physical methods in organic chemistry, organic synthesis, liquid crystals, the chemistry of natural products, high polymer chemistry, and heterocyclic chemistry. (Significantly, no undergraduate courses in business are required.)

Given the need to differentiate itself from the neighboring Wharton School at the University of Pennsylvania and the desirability of enrolling well-prepared science graduates, the Temple School of Business and Management added the new chemistry concentration with little, if any, objection from the business faculty. Since the program has yet to attract large numbers of students, perhaps because of the death of its founder or a lack of aggressive marketing, only time will tell whether it succeeds or fails.

In place of a concentration in a technical area, the Johnson School

---

[19] Taken from "The M.B.A. in Chemistry" announcement, Temple University, Philadelphia, Pa.

of Management at Cornell University is inviting young professionals holding master's or Ph.D. degrees in scientific or technical fields to enroll in a twelve-month foreshortened M.B.A. option which, except for a compressed core curriculum, is standard. The program, which began with twenty-five students in June 1995, includes three students with master's degrees in chemistry and engineering, and two with Ph.D.s in zoology and chemistry. It is assumed, says John Elliott who spear-headed the program, that because of their analytical background and proven skills in quantitative methods, such young professionals will be able to do most of the core curriculum of a traditional M.B.A. program in a single summer. Once they join the second-year class in the fall, however, their program will be indistinguishable from the rest. Essentially, the twelve-month option allows academic credit for these students' previous graduate training.

There are no plans at Cornell to advance the science student's technical knowledge base in science or to engage the technical student as a teaching resource for the other M.B.A. candidates. Cornell's program, however, is more than a marketing strategy for gaining new M.B.A. candidates by offering a shorter and less expensive route to the degree. By incorporating and recognizing the strengths of students with technical and scientific backgrounds, the school is taking one step toward new ways of credentialing students as practitioners of science. In contrast, Temple's approach (although its future is uncertain) is more far-reaching because it acknowledges the importance of continued graduate training in science as an integral part of the master's in business.

Building on an existing major in science not housed in any individual department, the trustees of Penn State approved in March 1995 a five-year, science-business B.S.-M.B.A. program proposed jointly by the Eberly College of Science and the Smeal College of Business. The program is modeled on the university's highly successful Jefferson program for premedical students, another accelerated offering. In addition to meeting requirements for the B.S. in science (a broad, general science degree with options in the physical, mathematical, or life sciences), the ten to twelve students who enroll in the program will take two semesters of economics and one each of accounting and statistics as a core of business-related courses during their first three years. Two summer co-op programs will also be assigned, the first in technical sales and product development, the second in a technical area within a customer service center. The summer co-ops will be followed in both years by a group seminar on campus as a way of "magnifying" students' experiences. The term is Donald Genson's, a chemist for twenty-one years with the Dow Chemical Company, who has joined Penn State as executive director of the new program. Other innovations include pairing each student with a corporate mentor, and industry-designed and taught courses throughout the five-year program.[20]

"Major developments and trends in both the corporate and academic science sectors," reads Penn State's proposal, "have conspired to make the development of an academic program that weaves together the cultures of scientific research and technical management an idea whose time has come. . . . It is intended that graduates . . . will be 'fast track,' future business managers who can successfully bridge the connections between technology and business change."[21] Penn State undergraduates already have the opportunity to apply to schools of medicine or dentistry after their sophomore year and, if accepted, enter professional school after their junior year. The new B.S.-M.B.A. program is similar in structure and proposes to attract and select "excellent students with defined career goals."

Perhaps as important as the graduates of the program, say its supporters, will be its spillover effects: "new knowledge about the science-management interface in U.S. corporations and new organizational mechanisms to integrate technological and managerial strategies. Faculty and students in both science and business will become more aware of the need for science-business cross-training, and research topics built around this interface will begin to emerge."[22] New courses developed for the science B.S.-M.B.A. program are expected to be available to undergraduates in other fields. The program requires a high degree of direct industry participation and will create opportunities for industry and academic scientists to interact in research and other areas.

Afterthoughts

It is one thing to mount professional master's programs at a variety of institutions as a niche-filling strategy.[23] But it will be quite another feat to get the research-oriented science community to embrace such experiments or to find graduate faculty to teach in them. Faculty objections are easy to anticipate. An applications-oriented master's degree in science contradicts just about everything physical science faculty are rewarded for doing: It asks them to prepare students for careers

---

[20] Information about Penn State's new B.S.-M.B.A. program is taken from material provided to the authors by John Cahir, Penn State provost for undergraduate education, as augmented by Donald Genson in a conversation after the proposal was approved.

[21] From the "Proposal, Penn State University, Five-Year Science/Business BS/MBA Program," Feb. 25, 1995.

[22] Ibid.

[23] As recommended by the congressional Office of Technology Assessment in *Federally Funded Research: Decisions for a Decade* (Washington, D.C.: USGPO, May 1991), pp. 226-227.

unlike their own, to develop skills other than those appreciated by specialized researchers, and to revalue what a master's degree is or should be, apart from a way stop on the road to the Ph.D.

Even if these objections can be overcome, we are left with an issue that may be just as thorny: who will support the students who enroll in these programs? Graduate fellowships are few in number and pretty much limited to future Ph.D.s. Is it appropriate to consider ways to tithe industry to support more industry-oriented, graduate-level training in science? Or will industry prefer to do the continuing education of employees on its own?

Revitalizing Undergraduate Programs in Science

Even scientist-educators favorably inclined to multi- or interdisciplinary postgraduate training insist that it be built on a strong set of skills gained in a single discipline at the undergraduate level.[24] Hence, there may be more resistance to tinkering with undergraduate education in the physical sciences than to changing graduate training. A more forward-looking perspective is demonstrated by the American Chemical Society's recent approval of multiple tracks in the undergraduate curriculum and interdisciplinary areas that include chemistry. Even more changes may be needed in undergraduate physics if new kinds of science professionals are to stimulate new demands for their services.

Two Surveys

Werner Wolf, chair of the applied physics department at Yale, recently conducted a survey to determine the extent to which changes are being contemplated in undergraduate and some graduate programs in physics.[25] Wolf's survey began with a questionnaire mailed to ninety colleges and universities, and was followed by telephone interviews with another twenty-five. Half those surveyed were topflight four-year colleges, with the balance divided between universities ranked highly by the National Academy of Sciences, or institutions with applied or engineering physics programs. Some 69 percent of the colleges and 52 percent of the universities responded. Questions concerning students' postbaccalaureate careers documented what many have known for a long time: physics students successfully pursue a wide range of career paths. But in the responses to his questionnaires, Wolf found that academic physicists are not ready for a change in outlook.[26] A typical re-

---

[24] This point was made strongly by both Harry Gray, chemist at Caltech, and Marvin Goldberger, a physicist now at UCSD, in personal communications to the authors.

[25] Werner P. Wolf, "Is Physics Education Adapting," p. 51.

sponse from Ned Rouze, a physics professor at Hope College, described the teaching faculty as "pure" physicists who tend to expose students only to their way of doing science. Something must be done, Rouze wrote, to increase the awareness of professors to careers outside the classical path.

Wolf specifically wanted to explore the way the pure versus applied science gap is perceived by faculty and students, and how it affects curriculum decisions. A surprising response was received to a set of questions on courses taken by undergraduate physics majors at four-year colleges. The surprise was how few students took practical courses: computer science was taken by only 3% of undergraduate physics majors, biophysics by 2%, and the physics of fluids was taken by 1%.[27] In some institutions, small enrollments had resulted in such courses being dropped.

Marketing (or its absence) came in for comment in the above and other contexts. Undergraduates are usually not told that physics majors make the better engineering graduate students, commented survey respondent David Nolte of Purdue University. "The perception that only engineering will provide students with the skills to land a more promising job . . . is definitely a danger to physics programs," he wrote.[28] The reason faculty behavior is hard to change came through in the Wolf report: "The majority of respondents felt that their present programs for undergraduates were quite successful and needed no significant changes."[29]

Werner Wolf is not the only science educator concerned about the relevance and utility of the undergraduate program. Chemist Philip Chenier wants more courses in polymer chemistry. "If as many as 50 percent of industrial chemists are involved with synthetic polymers (as some say), and very few undergraduate programs offer courses in polymers, the needs of a good many future chemists are not being met," he says.[30]

When we embarked on our own survey, we were mindful that over the years a whole host of experiments in alternate undergraduate science education had been tried and abandoned. As one example, we met graduates of Cornell University's long abandoned physics "option B" (not unlike the B.A. in the old B.A.-B.S. dichotomy) for those not bound for graduate school. In some places the B.A. science degree has fallen on hard times, but elsewhere established and well-supported

[26] Ibid., p. 54.

[27] Wolf, "Is Physics Education Adapting," p. 49.

[28] Ibid.

[29] Ibid., p. 50.

[30] For more information see Philip J. Chenier, University of Wisconsin-Eau Claire, "Preparing Students for Industry: A Different Approach to Undergraduate Research," *Council on Undergraduate Research Quarterly* (Mar. 1995).

bachelor of arts programs are attracting a wider range of students to science, and new B.A. programs appear to be coming on line. At the University of North Carolina at Chapel Hill, for example, fully one-half of the physics majors take the B.A. instead of the B.S. At Dickinson College in Pennsylvania, the physics department is seeking support for a new majors' curriculum involving project-centered, upper-division physics courses on topics such as magnetic resonance imaging in medicine, solar power generation, digital studio recording, chaos in weather, the potential dangers of radon in the environment, plasma particle motion, and cosmology.[31]

Expansion may involve compression and some compromise in the traditional requirements. At the University of Arkansas as of 1996, the department of physics will offer a new bachelor of arts degree beginning with algebra-based (instead of calculus-based) introductory physics, and requiring a three-course, upper-division sequence in another (nonphysics) field. The new program is designed to attract pre-education, prebusiness, and prelaw students to what physics professor Art Hobson, speaking personally, calls "our present anemic, professionally-oriented bachelor's degree" in physics. Indeed, in recent years at Arkansas as at many other Research I universities, there have been more graduate students than undergraduate majors in the university's physics program.[32]

Since, as far as we could tell in our modest survey of new programs in undergraduate science, there were no consistent patterns, the examples that follow are roughly categorized as: (1) enhanced traditional; (2) dual majors, or majors with "strong minors"; and (3) interdisciplinary and applied.

Enhanced Traditional

Many science educators are beginning to talk about enhancing, enlarging, or restructuring existing programs in the physical sciences. One recommendation specifically for physics comes from Marvin Goldberger, former president of Caltech, who notes that the last two years of the physics major tend to consist of "finer and more sophisticated derivations of everything," good preparation for graduate school but not for much else.[33] In place of such courses, Goldberger would have physics majors learn "applications of physical principles to the widest

---

[31] From the Jun. 1994 grant application to NSF from Dickinson, shared with the authors.

[32] Descriptions and quotation taken from a personal communication to the authors from Art Hobson, professor of physics at the University of Arkansas, Fayetteville.

[33] Marvin Goldberger, "A Twenty-First Century Physics Department" (talk given at the winter meeting of the AAPT, San Diego, Calif., Jan. 1994). Quoted with Goldberger's permission.

possible range of problems, developing and deepening the theory as one goes along."[34] He has, as mentioned earlier, fifty such problems in mind out of which semester-long courses for physics majors (and graduate students) could be constructed.

Chemistry, which more than physics provides a significant work force for industry, has already taken some steps toward legitimizing a more varied undergraduate curriculum. In 1989, the ACS Committee on Professional Training (CPT) enlarged its curriculum guidelines to include several alternate tracks through an ACS-approved chemistry major. It is now possible to offer and take ACS-approved concentrations in biochemistry (by far the most popular option to date), polymer chemistry, chemical education, and a few others.[35] Reduction in the core requirements also means that chemistry majors today have room in their curriculum for genetics, molecular biology, and environmental science, perhaps even business and psychology, in their fourth year.

But new curricula do not necessarily change the culture. "The large research universities," says Elizabeth Ivey, a physicist and former provost at Macalester College, "still give the impression that the only undergraduate of value is the one who's going on to become a principal investigator."[36] Ivey, who taught at Smith College for many years, found it possible to provide her physics majors with some engineering classes without turning them into engineers. She and her colleagues negotiated with the University of Massachusetts and Dartmouth to allow Smith students to substitute certain engineering courses for their required physics courses. "With a little engineering under their belts," she reports, her students had more success in competing for industrial jobs. This corresponds to the prediction by many that in the next century science and engineering will converge.

Similarly convergent, one could argue, will be science and business. Duncan Moore, APS Congressional Fellow and professor of physics at the University of Rochester, is "convinced," as he writes in *Physics Today*, that "scientists can [and by inference should] learn the few things they need to know in order to make a good business decision, or to judge whether [a certain] technology stands a chance to profit a company in a certain time frame."[37] Physicists at Moorhead State (see below) could not agree more.

---

[34] Ibid.

[35] As outlined by the Committee on the Study of Chemistry Education in the U.S., 1989, as reported to the authors by David K. Lavallee. The committee had as its mandate recommendations for improving precollege chemistry, college chemistry, and continuing education for professional chemists; graduate education was later assigned (1993) to the Lavallee Task Force.

[36] Elizabeth Ivey, personal communication to the authors.

[37] Duncan Moore, quoted in "Reinventing the Future," p. 30.

The "Strong Minor" and Dual Majors

Moorhead's physics with business minor is the result of discussions by a forward-looking physics chair with the dean of the business school. Concerned equally with the employability of Moorhead's physics majors and their diminishing number, Vijendra Agarwal is modeling his program on those at a number of state universities, notably the University of Wisconsin-Eau Claire, that feature chemistry with business minors.[38]

"Chem-biz," so-called, was introduced at UW-Eau Claire in 1973 and has so far graduated 241 students, 90 percent of whom have been placed in industrial positions. The major requires thirty-three credit hours in chemistry, including an applied physical chemistry course instead of the standard physical chemistry, and courses on the chemical industry and on industrial chemistry. Chem-biz students compete successfully with business majors, says Phil Chenier, chem-biz adviser, because of their technical training; they compete successfully with chemical engineers and chemistry majors because of their strong minor in business and economics. Chem-biz majors have been employed in over 130 different companies, with twenty-three hiring two or more.[39]

Agarwal hopes "phys-biz" will accomplish a number of goals at Moorhead: (1) increase the employability of physics majors not planning graduate study in physics; (2) increase the attractiveness of the physics undergraduate major, especially for women and minorities; and (3) make the graduating major a more competitive applicant to professional schools and postgraduate programs.[40] Agarwal and his department insist that phys-biz will be a physics major with a business minor and not a business degree. To this end, new courses in physics are being developed on such topics as physics of materials science, optical and electrical properties of materials, and instrumentation. More sophisticated versions of traditional business courses, legal issues in regulation, for example, will be offered for phys-biz majors with calculus background.

Increased employability can come from courses other than business. For chemistry and physics majors, some credits in biology may provide just that breadth employers are looking for. Given the prominence of biotechnology in current industry R&D, a few physical scientists are beginning to try to develop links to the life sciences, if not yet a full-fledged physics degree with biology minor. Traditionally, biology stu-

---

[38] See the discussion of "chem-biz" at UW-Eau Claire in Sheila Tobias, *Revitalizing Undergraduate Science: Why Some Things Work and Most Don't* (Tucson, Ariz.: Research Corporation, 1992), pp. 30-31.

[39] Philip J. Chenier, "Preparing Students," p. 147.

[40] Unpublished plan for the new minor provided the authors by Vijendra Agarwal.

dents have been required to take some physics and chemistry. In the new model, physics and chemistry students will be encouraged to take one or more courses in biology. As a quid pro quo, the required physics and chemistry courses for biology majors could be reworked to cover topics that are immediately relevant to the life sciences.[41]

Such a plan is in the offing for physics, but not yet either approved or funded at Humboldt State University. Taking advantage of the reinstatement of a required physics course for biology majors, Richard Stepp, chair of physics, is proposing a tailor-made, physics-for-biology-majors course in place of traditional introductory mechanics. His hope is to interest biology students in such topics as thermodynamics and fluid mechanics, usually not introduced until late in the standard physics curriculum, and to attract some number of them either to a physics minor or to a joint degree. Initially the course would be offered to a virtually captive audience of biology and natural resources majors. Eventually, in a three-course or four-course sequence, the "physics of biology" might provide an important minor for both physics majors and biologists, even a way of increasing the number of physics majors (there are currently only twenty-five at Humboldt State, compared to 700 in the life sciences).[42] Marvin Goldberger would have *every* physics and chemistry major take a course in the life sciences. Goldberger and Stepp may be paving the way for a revitalized general science degree, one that would stress "well-rounded" as well as "well-grounded" in a family of disciplines.

Noting that premedical students rarely major in physics because of the burden of their biology and chemistry requirements, the department of physics at Georgetown University (as of the 1994-95 academic year) is offering a new option expressly designed for students planning to attend medical school. This option will allow premeds to substitute two semesters' credit in general chemistry and two semesters' credit in organic chemistry for three upper-level physics electives and a senior thesis in the standard physics major. At Georgetown as in Arkansas (page 102), an algebra-based introductory physics course may replace the calculus-based course as the first course taken in the major sequence. Apart from lessening the requirements for the physics major, the new option will permit premedical students to make the choice for physics as late as their sophomore year.[43]

---

[41] See one such curriculum, intended for premedical students at Harvard, linking certain topics in physics and chemistry to biochemistry. Sheila Tobias, *Revitalizing*, chap. 6.

[42] Richard Stepp, personal communication to the authors.

[43] Further information about Georgetown's premed physics option is available from Professor Joseph McClure and a world-wide-web page at httpp://www.physics.georgetown.edu/Premed.html.

In all its history Harvey Mudd College has never awarded a degree for any major outside of science and engineering. But in an effort to invent another variant of the science-trained professional, the trustees of the college are considering a proposal to allow students to major in such outside fields (indeed, outside of the college itself) as political science, sociology, and English among others. The only limitations would be that they complete fifty hours of science at Harvey Mudd and one or more technical minors. In some ways, the new degree is easier to implement at Harvey Mudd than elsewhere, since the college is part of the Claremont (California) Colleges which together offer a wide range of liberal arts courses and majors. Still, the proposal is a radical departure from past practice, since the college will be offering a B.S. in engineering to students with only a science core and technical minors, albeit skills and knowledge in other diverse areas. Cross-fertilization is an expected benefit: Harvey Mudd students have always taken electives at the neighboring liberal arts campuses. Now some will be more permanent fixtures, interacting with (and no doubt educating) their fellow majors.[44]

Interdisciplinary and Applied Science

"General science" may turn out to be "applied science" in its twenty-first-century incarnation if a newly instituted science program at the University of North Carolina at Chapel Hill is an indicator. Designed to prepare students for careers in the scientific and technological professions, either directly or following graduate school, the program has a prominent focus on materials science. It distinguishes itself both from the traditional science major and from the traditional engineering curriculum in several ways.[45] Unlike the pure sciences, it offers five specific tracks, one in computer science and four in different areas of materials science: biomedical, polymeric, physics-based, and chemistry-based. What distinguishes the program from engineering is its *flexibility*. Majors are interchangeable as late as the junior year. The program appears to follow the Goldberger dictum: After the foundation courses, scientific principles can be learned just as well by means of applications as by further theoretical study.

What stands out from the list of courses for each track is the degree of integration. The biomedical materials track requires physics, mechanics through modern physics, and then some. What we are seeing in Chapel Hill's applied sciences option is close to a two- or even three-

---

[44] Information about the proposed program came from a personal communication with Sheldon Wettack, vice president and dean of the faculty at Harvey Mudd.

[45] See *Carolina and the Sciences*, University of North Carolina at Chapel Hill Office of Public Affairs, 1994 edition.

field general science degree focused on processes and products just coming into wide use. Evidence for its broad applicability is that the program is not being taken by materials science students alone. It is being marketed to premed, prelaw, pre-engineering, and environmental science preprofessionals as well. Potential students are reminded in the program announcement that—as one example—"patent and technical law is a demanding and rewarding career, but few lawyers have legal *and* technical experience."[46]

Multiple tracks in the physics major diversify and integrate the sciences at Murray State University in Kentucky. According to physics chair Steve Cobb, these tracks (called "areas" at Murray State) are the reason the university boasts between 80 and 100 undergraduate physics majors when comparable institutions settle for fifteen. Thirty-five students pursue the traditional physics curriculum, about thirty-five a modified engineering physics curriculum, ten are in a pre-engineering program, and ten are pre-optometry students. Murray State's areas are similar to the concentrations within physics (computer science, biophysics) used by other departments to broaden their curricula.[47]

Particularly unusual is Murray State's flexibility in all areas of physics. Students can switch areas during their four years. They can elect minors in business for management careers, or in English for careers in technical writing. Some use physics in preparation for law school. The curriculum is even broad enough to allow these physics and engineering physics majors to work in nearby chemical industries. Indeed, engineering physics includes calculus-based chemistry (ten hours), computer science, statics, heat transfer, and electro-optics. Cobb and his colleagues say their students "learn a little bit about a lot of things," which enables them to find a niche when they graduate.

Murray State's physics program is atypical. Although it is not part of an engineering school, Cobb says, "putting the name 'engineering' into the major makes our graduates more appealing to employers." Indeed, since 1978, the program has graduated 350 in physics, of which 185 were in engineering physics.[48] One of the reasons Murray State's physics department may be comfortable being less "purist" than others is that several of the faculty come from industry. All have Ph.D.s in physics, but like Cobb, who came to Murray State from McDonnell Douglas, they are more willing than faculty elsewhere to see their majors enter industry. The lesson to be taken from Murray State's program is that the undergraduate physics major can be competitive with engineer-

---

[46] Ibid., p. 2.

[47] Wolf, "Is Physics Education Adapting," p. 49.

[48] Steve Cobb, personal communication to the authors.

ing—even in a tight job market—if the program is well matched to the needs of students and of industry.[49]

Tentative Conclusions

The new programs described here notwithstanding, most undergraduates majoring in physics or chemistry don't have the opportunity to pursue an enhanced, dual, or applied major, or to add a nontraditional minor to their program. Nor do fields such as science journalism yet exist at the baccalaureate level in science departments. The barriers work both ways. Departments of social science, even those aiming to place their graduates in public policy positions (environmental and health), don't recommend dual majors with natural science.

Chemist Harry Gray insists that "there is a need for science-trained people in every occupation."[50] In an uncertain market, those prepared in a science-based discipline (or disciplinary hybrid) should be afforded more employment opportunities, not less. But until undergraduate programs in science appeal to and serve the generalist, the niche for alternative science programs in the academy will continue to lag behind the emergent demand for "new scientists" in the world of work.

---

[49] There are, in addition to the programs described above, about 90 "technology" or "industrial science" B.S. programs in the U.S. approved by the Accrediting Board for Engineering and Technology. For the most part outgrowths and enlargements of two-year technology programs, they have potential to provide advanced education in science and technology. But they demand too few science courses of their enrollees (typically only one year of chemistry or physics) and are not yet real alternatives to the B.S. or B.A. degree in science.

[50] Harry Gray, personal communication to the authors.

7

Conclusion

RESTRUCTURING DEMAND

W HAT is America's stake in American science? How do we measure
it? And how do we convince employers, the general public, and
Congress itself that science is valuable, not just for the products it offers, but for the possibilities it engenders? Along with curiosity-driven
research, applied problems, as Robert Sproull used to tell his Ph.D.
students, "deserve our respect." Both types of research require a strong
scientific infrastructure, sustained funding from a variety of sources,
and a steady supply of new talent. If the vagaries of supply and demand
are to be replaced with strong and certain career pathways for science-
trained professionals, we will have to explore new ways of restructuring demand. In this chapter we begin that exploration in a way that is
more suggestive than comprehensive. We are optimistic because, contrary to much current opinion, we believe not only that scientific skills will
be increasingly vital in the years ahead, but that there is a reservoir of good
will for science that has yet to be tapped. Restructuring demand for scientific expertise will draw on that reservoir and all of our skills.

The Federal Role

The federal government is partly responsible for the supply of scientists. Why shouldn't it be partly responsible for the demand? Since Sput-
nik production of new scientists has been supported with federal R&D
funding (a proxy for private sector demand). From 1959 to 1971, according to the Office of Technology Assessment, this support resulted
in a boom in doctoral production.[1] In fact, until the Apollo program
was scaled back in 1967, increasing federal support of academic R&D
(by 20 percent annually in constant dollars) swelled the number of
graduate students on federal fellowships and traineeships. Ph.D. awards

---

[1] This and what follows derives from U.S. Congress, Office of Technology Assessment, *Higher Education for Science and Engineering* (Washington, D.C.: USGPO, Mar. 1989), pp. 126-128.

109

declined only after fellowships were cut back in 1969, despite high undergraduate enrollments. The point to stress is this: a federally-induced market for researchers drove Ph.D. production, not private sector demand or changing demographics.

The boom subsided—as they all must—when the demand for more R&D and a supporting infrastructure (faculty expansion and university development) had been met. As OTA reported it,

> [By the mid-1970s] social and political priorities shifted away from cold-war-inspired science . . . . By 1974, the proportion of graduate students relying on federal support had dropped from 40% (the 1969 peak) to 25%. Engineering and physical science were the most affected. Fellowships and traineeships dropped 90% from 13,600 in 1969 to 1,500 in 1975, and at NASA, DOD, and the Atomic Energy Commission [a forerunner of DOE] research funds dropped 45% in real terms.[2]

The demand spiral reversed itself again in the late 1970s and early 1980s when computer, semiconductor, and energy markets surged. Engineering was the main beneficiary in university enrollments, while overall the number of graduate students with federal support continued to decline.[3]

This historical vignette suggests that the federal role has been to target research problems and protect scientists by insulating them from short-term market forces. Yet, despite these important contributions, the federal government is damned at every turn: if it rescues declining fields through graduate student support, it is accused of mindlessly investing in a supply which will overwhelm demand. If, on the other hand, it responds too vigorously to market signals in new fields, it can amplify the shortsightedness of employers and rob science of a well-distributed (by discipline) base of new graduates. And if it does *nothing* in fields in which the U.S. appears to be losing its lead, it is accused of undermining economic competitiveness.

We believe there are ways of revising government mechanisms to restructure demand. If federally-supported graduate research assistants and postdocs could be made more independent of their sponsors (as John Armstrong, Truman Schwartz, and others believe they should; see chapter 5), they could pursue productive lines of inquiry on their own and perhaps become immediately employable upon graduation. Fellowships are one way of shifting control of graduate studies to students; traineeships vest such control in institutions. Both types of sup-

---

[2] Ibid., p. 128.

[3] Ibid., p. 129.

port could be invigorated, as was recommended by several of the industrial recruiters we queried (see page 56).

Typically, federal support for graduate students is filtered through an array of research programs, irrespective of how these programs enhance the employment prospects of those being trained. Whole areas of research continue to exist while new areas grow up around them. As a result, young scientists (as we have seen in their responses to the current job market) are unprepared for the fickleness of opportunity and the possibility that their training may be mismatched to future funding. Knowing future funding priorities would be, of course, the best way to predict demand. Harry Wasserman, an organic chemist at Yale University, thinks future demand will be stimulated not by "finding new sources of money to support scientists," but "by finding new science for scientists to do," such as "green chemistry" (preventative environmentalism), which applies chemicals at the catalytic instead of at the stoichiometric levels to reduce toxic waste, cascade reactions, and so on.[4]

Another government mechanism for maintaining science and scientists has been the national labs. Historically, the "Big Five" were heavily involved in weapons-related research, but others made significant non-military contributions to basic science by supporting large-scale instrumentation that universities could not afford. With the end of the cold war, the pressure is on to recalculate the value of all the labs in terms of the economy. Some of their supporters are eager to redefine their missions in terms of dual-use technologies, innovations purported to fulfill defense and civilian needs simultaneously.[5] But another approach is to view the labs as a reservoir (albeit an expensive one) of talent and experience.[6] Even if we are justified in asking the federal government to help sustain or restructure demand for scientists, can we link the national labs to the long-term health of science and technology? And do the labs represent the best use of captive talent at current budget levels? Absent pressing military priorities, the national labs could be considered a long-term labor support system. But who will decide whether this is worth doing and how many scientists are "enough?" At a time when the nation's twenty-seven national laboratories and federal research facilities are coming under review, the question is timely.

---

[4] Harry Wasserman, personal communication to the authors. See also "Chemists Clean Up Synthesis with One-Pot Reactions," *Science* 266 (7 Oct. 1994): pp. 32-33.

[5] For a contrasting view, see the widely-reported Galvin Report on alternative futures for the DOE national laboratories presented to Congress, Feb.24, 1995. The commission, led by Robert Galvin, chairman of the board of Motorola, indicated its reluctance to support the dual-use concept as reported in *Science* 267 (27 Jan. 1995): pp. 446-447.

[6] In other countries, such as Germany, national labs are not agency-administered or mission-dependent, but are engaged in the support of basic research.

The Role of the Private Sector

What is the role of commerce and industry in matching scientific expertise to jobs? A slew of legislative and executive initiatives encourage corporate collaboration with public and private universities, national laboratories, and state government. But truth be told, incentives such as the Stevenson-Wydler Technology Innovation Act of 1980 (reauthorized more than once) to confer tax credits for private investment in R&D have never had much impact. Either the federal government is considered too unreliable a partner (tax credits may not remain in force from one session of Congress to another), or corporations don't want to risk their R&D portfolios by collaborating with outsiders. A third reason may be that the tax advantage, as permitted by the Congress, is calculated only on *increases* in research expenditures, not on the actual cost of maintaining research.

Many aspects of market demand for scientific personnel were touched on in the proceedings of a symposium held in Washington, D.C. in July, 1992.[7] Industry operates within a new set of constraints, participants were told. Set in a global marketplace that is stratified by sector, companies must increasingly rely on multidisciplinary solutions to science-based problems. In addition, finite resources require technological organizations to stay within well-planned objectives over longer time frames. Within those constraints, however, the demand for technically-trained personnel who can do multiple tasks and learn others quickly is growing. When companies fail to locate the "complete package" in any one professional ("gold-collar workers," as Curt Mathews of Rohm and Haas calls them), they will rate new applicants on intellectual agility, versatility, and receptivity to new tasks. But how can such multiple skills be introduced into graduate education? Perhaps industry-university collaboration can be justified as much as a training incubator as a way of producing knowledge.

Alternate Careers in the Private Sector

There was a flurry of excitement in 1993-94 when a small number of Ph.D. physicists found their way to Wall Street. Their ability to understand "derivatives" in the market (derivatives are highly leveraged instruments whose value is linked to the performance of other assets) made them a "hot item" (and generated a *Time* magazine cover story), at least for a while. More relevant is the quieter story of physicists who went into the venture capital industry over the past two decades. Rather than on Wall Street, they were more likely to be found on the San

---

[7] *Preparing for the 21st Century: Human Resources in Science and Technology* (Washington, D.C.: Commission on Professionals in Science and Technology, Jul. 1992).

Francisco peninsula or in Boston with companies like Advanced Technology Ventures. The derivatives story notwithstanding, the possibility that scientists can be valued, indeed prized, for their unique competencies underscores their (and our) interest in increasing the demand for their expertise in other sectors of the economy.

But who will train these scientists for business? Since few companies are eager to retrain,[8] it is all the more important that today's young scientists figure out what industry wants. This means, says John Armstrong, they have to study the industry in general, the would-be employer in depth, and make a convincing case that their skills and background will fit in and enhance the company's efforts.[9] Scientists aren't used to selling themselves in this fashion and business isn't set up to employ science-trained professionals in other arenas.[10] So, there is much to be learned on both sides.

Another arena for more immediate hiring of science-trained professionals in the private sector is manufacturing technology. The stagnation of American industry, wrote Robert Reich in 1983, ten years before he became secretary of labor, was the result of "the management era," when business school graduates, trained in marketing, management, and finance but with no particular technical background, were running American business.[11] If science and engineering converge in the future, as Lewis M. Branscomb predicts,[12] then scientists exposed to the technical problems industries face might provide an attractive new engineering-management cadre.

It is tempting to jump on the "quality management" bandwagon and say, as Reich implies, that American business and industry would be better off with fewer lawyers, financial specialists, and traditional managers, and more science-trained professionals. Bandwagon or not, we agree. An untapped pool can bring new inspiration to business. But, the science community cannot simply wait for future employers to come knocking. To cap-

---

[8] Bellcore is an exception. Bellcore's contribution over the past few years has been to put more than 400 Ph.D. researchers (physicists and electrical engineers) through an expensive three-week crash course in software and systems engineering. See "In Sink-or-Swim Environment, Physicists Retrain to Survive," *Science* 261 (24 Sept. 1993): p. 1672.

[9] John Armstrong, personal communication to the authors. See also Peter Feibelman's advice to scientists, *A Ph.D. Is Not Enough: A Guide to Survival in Science* (Menlo Park, Calif.: Addison-Wesley, 1993).

[10] Vijendra Agarwal of Moorhead State's physics department found it hard to identify the personnel officer to talk to at large companies like Honeywell and 3-M about placement of prospective "physics with business minors." One office handles hiring of scientists, another hiring of marketing and management trainees. Agarwal's graduates would fall between the two.

[11] Robert Reich, *The Next American Frontier* (New York: Viking Penguin, 1983).

[12] Lewis M. Branscomb, personal communication to the authors.

italize on demand, it needs to prepare both itself and the next generation of scientists for work in alternate careers. In addition to urging large corporations to support in-house laboratories, academic science should try to demonstrate to private enterprise how useful science graduates can be in business roles away from the bench. This is where restructured supply—a repackaging, if you will—meets restructured demand.

The Self-Employed Scientist

Some science-trained professionals are making it as entrepreneurs. But in response to our questions about alternative futures, few scientists—even those who are unemployed—listed self-employment as an option. In other professions a period of self-employment, as a lawyer in private practice or an educator in consulting, for example, can help a person survive down times or career disruptions. Two things militate against self-employment for scientists: the need for laboratory facilities and the stimulation of a peer group. These might be mitigated by start-up loans and by access to computer networks and bulletin boards. But another barrier lies in attitudes and perceptions. Except for the senior scientist who builds an off-site business to develop some spill-over technology from research, part-time or self-generated employment tends not to be valued in science.

According to recent surveys, more and more Americans are finding their way into self-employment. While many of these would-be entrepreneurs will not make it financially and will eagerly accept employee status when jobs become available, their periods outside of a salary-paying organization will not necessarily be blots on their records. Until and unless the science community recognizes this kind of self-employment as legitimate and valuable, scientists in transition will have little option but to leave the field.

Academic Science: Placement and Matching Systems

If, as the American Physical Society reports, 800 U.S. or green-card-holding Ph.D.s in physics were graduated annually in the past few years, and if there were 800 positions for Ph.D. physicists available per year in those years, then the problem of unemployment in physics may not have been one of oversupply, but rather a problem of matching people (and their subspecialties) to jobs. In a nation as vast as ours, with only ad hoc systems (essentially no system) to locate jobs for people or people for jobs, it is not surprising that 200 or more applicants respond to any advertised academic position, and that 199 must be turned down.

In the "bad old days," as women and minorities are quick to remind us, placement of science professionals was too often done informally by students' mentors in conversations with friends and colleagues. With the advent of equal opportunity hiring, however, there is now pressure to advertise job openings and the requirement that search committees at least appear to have diverse applicant pools. What has replaced the bad effects of the old system, if we are to believe anecdotal accounts from our respondents and conversations with search committees, is application-overkill thanks to word processing. The vast numbers of applicants per job (more in academe than in industry) are accounted for by the ease with which applicants can tailor and reproduce their résumés. Sometimes applicants do not even go to the trouble of finding out much about the jobs for which they are applying or whether they are even marginally qualified (see page 63).

What would it take to establish a placement clearinghouse for scientists across disciplines and subfields? Each of the professional associations does this to some extent, and the American Chemical Society, with its dual labor market (academic and industrial), may be the most conscientious. But for the young scientist who cannot afford to travel to meetings (the ACS does waive fees for unemployed members), publications and computer networking may have to suffice. Why not, then, a national matching and placement system similar to that used to assign medical residencies? Medical schools and the hospitals to which they send their graduates as residents have worked out a complicated matching system in which each graduating senior lists five residencies in rank order of preference. Looking over the applicants, the hospital programs select five of the group in their preference order. Then, in a monstrous one-day number-crunching, matching is done. This is most likely too draconian a model for the science community (bear in mind the medical residency "match" is only for one or two years), but something like it might be explored for filling postdoctoral openings.

Certainly some shift in responsibility for placement to graduate faculties is called for. Otherwise, what incentive (apart from kindness) is there for faculty members to try to explore alternate careers for students and work to increase their versatility? Harley A. Thronson, Jr., chairing the Bahcall Committee of the Astronomy and Astrophysics Society, recently concluded that for fifteen years there had been an overproduction of astronomers of 2 to 3 percent annually. Thronson's remedy was that the "fate of a department's past graduates, rather than the training of new ones, become a factor in evaluating grant proposals from any of its faculty members."[13] What's interesting about the idea is that astronomy departments (as well as individual mentors) would be motivated to pay attention to the placement of their graduates, for continued funding would depend on success. Thronson happened upon a

[13] Harley A. Thronson, Jr., "The Production of Astronomers: A Model for Future Surpluses," in *Publication of the Astronomical Society of the Pacific* 103 (Jan. 1991): pp. 90-94.

truth noted by many of our respondents: graduate professors may be inclined only to place their best students in postdoctoral positions as a way of propagating their own work. There is no collective obligation for the mentor or the department as a whole to place its graduates in jobs.

Giving graduate faculties more responsibility for placement may require training. How much do professors know about the job market? About alternative occupations for the scientists they train? How much do students know about these subjects? What kind and how much training would it take to make a young scientist more skilled at defining problems independently, even across disciplines?

Teaching Postdocs

In addition to conventional postdoctoral appointments, *teaching postdocs* might profitably occupy (if only temporarily) pedagogically oriented scientists. With an oversupply of Ph.D. scientists and an undersupply of instructors at large state universities (particularly in lower-division physics and chemistry courses), one- to three-year teaching apprenticeships might be a worthy program for NSF or other federal agencies to support. Two models have been tried with some success. Since 1988 the Camille and Henry Dreyfus Foundation has been supporting about ten doctoral scientists per year as teaching postdocs at undergraduate colleges. In each instance the postdoc is teamed with a scholar who directs, inspires, and supervises the new instructor. The fellow benefits from an opportunity to try both teaching and research in a college setting. The mentor benefits from the assistance of a research-oriented Ph.D. who would not normally be available at the college. The cost to the foundation is $50,000 for two years of work, and an additional research start-up grant at the end if the recipient decides to pursue a career in college teaching.[14]

In a similar program, a science education consortia used part of its Pew Charitable Trust funding in the late 1980s to match up postdocs with participating institutions. Faculty of these institutions were relieved of one-half of their course loads in exchange for training and supervising a teaching postdoc. One Ph.D. who took advantage of this opportunity, geologist David Smith, is now running a teaching-learning center at LaSalle University in Philadelphia—a fitting and unconventional career step he was emboldened to take because of his teaching postdoc at Colorado College. A "teaching postdoc" need not be a formal arrangement. While chairman of physics at the University of Chicago, Hellmut Fritzsche reduced the department's use of first- and sec-

---

[14] Robert Lichter, executive director, and Harry Wasserman, Dreyfus Foundation board member, personal communications to the authors.

ond-year graduate students as teaching assistants by using postdocs and older graduate students instead. The benefits were mutual: the grad students and research associates gained valuable teaching experience; students had more mature instructors in class.[15]

There's always the risk, Smith and others say, that teaching postdocs may never find their way back to research. But the desperate need for dynamic science instructors, especially in state universities, is reason to consider expansion of the Dreyfus and Pew models with other sources of funding.

Survival During Voluntary and Involuntary Career Interruptions

We cannot conclude a survey of career prospects in science without making a plea for the scientist whose career is interrupted either by family responsibilities (voluntary) or by years' long inability to get a permanent job (involuntary). Geologist Cathy Manduca is a case in point. Manduca holds a Ph.D. in geology from Caltech. Her current "underemployment," as she likes to call it, is the result of a combination of family responsibilities (two small children) and geographical limitations. Manduca is faced with three challenges: first, how to function as a scientist—that is, to continue to do research—during a period of underemployment; second, how eventually to reenter the job market with a viable curriculum vitae after even a temporary disruption. "Finally," she writes, "it has been important to maintain my self-esteem. And this has been the hardest to do."[16]

To maintain herself as a scientist, Manduca negotiated a position as a continuing research associate at a nearby college that allowed her to write proposals for funding, provided office space, and included access to a research library and some laboratory equipment. She also arranged to do research in laboratories out of state by being in residence for short stints, and at a local business. To stay in contact with the scientific community (and to hear about other research opportunities), she has continued to go to scientific meetings even though she is unable to give papers with her previous frequency.

What is making all this possible, why Manduca is surviving professionally where others in her situation would not, is that her spouse has helped pay for child care, Manduca's trips to meetings and laboratories, and office maintenance costs. To assist others, Manduca suggests

---

[15] Hellmut Fritzsche, personal communication to the authors.

[16] The quotations and details come from a memo, written to the authors to answer their queries, and are quoted with Cathy Manduca's permission.

establishment of a support program to make it easier for part-time scientists to maintain membership in the professional community for two- to five-year periods. At the very least, productive scientists wishing to return to research after a voluntary or involuntary interruption ought to be eligible for start-up support.

How much would it take to extend placement services to the part-time scientist? To inform local business and industry when someone with a particular kind of training moves into a region? To accommodate scientists in transition on site or during extended working visits at the national labs? At university-industry consortia? It is tempting to dismiss proposals like these as just more entitlement programs at a time when scientists ought to be cutting back on supply, not maintaining it. But the cost of un- or underemployment in science is heavy, both to society which loses trained people and to individuals attempting to keep up in rapidly changing fields.

One attractive feature of programs to help sustain un- and underemployed scientists would be the availability of trained professionals for short assignments. Scientists in transition could be made available to industry, perhaps through a registry, as "itinerant experts" who would bring specialized knowledge into new venues and bridge scientific disciplines. While such consultants are not uncommon at the most senior levels of academe and industry, they are relatively rare at the middle or lower levels where they may be more needed.

Career disruption is difficult professionally, financially, and psychologically, even when it is temporary. The possibility that a temporary disruption might result in a permanent derailment of a career makes the situation even more traumatic. When a scientist loses contact, momentum and confidence may vanish. A support plan would not only assist individuals to stay in science but would also permit the nation to salvage its investment in their training. To do less is to discourage not just the current generation from science, but future generations as well.

Calculating the Added Value of Science to Society

In selling science to the public, the department chair, the company recruiter, the congressional staffer, the agency program officer, and the national associations of scientists may have different priorities. But a more general view must prevail: Human resources in science are a national treasure that add value to the world. The issue of "added value" is the critical one. Anyone who understands the process by which the advanced economies of the world have moved from agriculture to manufacturing, and then to the production of knowledge along with goods and services, will agree at least in theory that science as a spur to technology adds value to the economy. But the quantitative measure of that added value is elusive. It is one thing to compute the value of the telecommunications industry in terms of sales and profits, exports, and employment (*new wealth*); it is quite another to compute the value of its knowledge base as a stimulus to economic growth, the numerous jobs (*new sources of wealth*) created by the new industries it has spawned, the higher efficiency of business in all sectors that it has made possible—not to mention improved quality of life. Without some measure of "added value" by science and technology to the economy and well-being of this nation, however, the argument for full employment of scientists (and what economists lump under the rubric of "human capital") remains a philosophical one at best.

A first order of business, then, for those who engage in science and technology policy is to attempt to compute, account for, and factor in the added value of science.[17] This involves analyses of the value to the economy of having, for example, the best advanced training in science in the world (affordability and limited access notwithstanding); the benefits to the economy in general that flow from technological innovation; the benefits overall, not just to the industries that profit from them, of advances in computers, lasers, global positioning satellites, automation, transportation, biotechnology, agriculture, and pharmaceuticals, as well as building materials and technologies, and telecommunications; what Jack Gibbons, the president's science adviser, calls in the aggregate science's "social rate of return."[18]

Such a calculation may seem daunting. But comparable valuations have been done in the recent past, and one economist (who won a Nobel Prize for the effort) has attempted to quantify (if only retrospectively) the direct benefits of education, research, and development to technological progress and to the economy.[19] The value of a pristine environment, to take an example from another hard-to-measure sector, is no longer calculated in terms of recreation alone. We measure health benefits and costs, along with new measures, such as the long-term availability (whether visited or not) of our nation's wilderness areas

---

[17] For example, see *Research Funding as an Investment: Can we Measure the Returns?* U.S. Congress, Office of Technology Assessment (Washington, D.C.: USGPO, April 1986). The short answer was "no."

[18] John H. Gibbons, address to a meeting on "Science in the National Interest," MIT, Feb. 7, 1995.

[19] According to economist Robert Solow's analysis, for much of the first half of this century, 80% of America's economic growth was due to "capital-independent technical progress"; 34% alone to "growth of knowledge" or what Solow calls "technical progress in its narrowest sense." See *Growth Theory: An Exposition*, Robert Solow's Nobel lecture (New York: Oxford University Press, 1987), p. 20. A commentator writes: "Solow's 1957 paper on technological progress changed the focus of growth economics from a crude emphasis on savings to a much-better appreciation of the importance of education, research, and development." Avinash Dixit, in *Growth, Productivity, and Unemployment: Essays to Celebrate Bob Solow's Birthday*, ed. Peter Diamond (Cambridge, Mass.: MIT Press, 1990), p.11.

and national parks (called by economists their "option value"). These have become part and parcel of the nation's land-planning metric.

Selling Science, Selling Scientists

An ideal future for science-trained professionals in the U.S. in the authors' opinion would look something like this: a significantly larger percentage of young people, regardless of race, ethnic background, gender, or disability, would be recruited to the study of science. Like today's ROTC and military academy candidates, they would be supported with tuition waivers, monthly stipends, and paid summer work experience. Those who chose to terminate their schooling with a two-year associate's degree would become technicians; those who continued in science through a B.S. or B.A. would not have to repay tuition waivers, no matter what their profession, because it would be understood by the public that science literacy is valuable in all sectors. Those earning degrees at the master's level would have opportunities to do meaningful science-related work. Those earning Ph.D.s would be employed at the bench or in the management of basic or applied research.

Lest this extension of the military-training model to science (mathematics and engineering might also be included) be considered too fanciful or rooted in the cold war, recall Vannevar Bush's original recommendation that 24,000 scholarships be given annually to undergraduates in science. Extending the military-training model still further, graduates in science (at all levels) would be expected to repay their fellowships with some form of science-related service in public institutions (schools, museums, hospitals, national labs), or in the private sector (industry, commerce, banks, environmental clean-up companies, law firms, media organizations).

This scenario assumes a population sympathetic to science, made up of both ordinary people and powerful decision-makers willing to pay for a science infrastructure. Just as the public willingly pays for "readiness" in the interest of national security, so it would greet scientific investigation ("scientific maneuvers," as it were) and a "science corps" of young graduates as investments in national long-term well-being. Some of the vanishing local and regional benefits of military spending (base employment and local contracts) would be resurrected by spending for science. Finally, the media in this ideal future would make science accessible, well-reported, intelligently criticized and, for the most part, celebrated as a national "good."[20]

Why does our scenario seem improbable? One answer common among scientists is that science illiteracy is so widespread in the pop-

---

[20] For an opinion on the importance of science writers to science, see William D. Carey, "Scientists and Sandboxes: Regions of the Mind," *American Scientist* 76 (Mar.-Apr. 1988): pp. 143-145.

ulation at large, and anti-scientism so virulent among a vocal few, as to subvert any appreciation that science might inspire.[21] In Washington it is generally believed that, apart from the space program, "there are no votes in science." This makes it even harder to imagine that the nation would happily sustain science-trained professionals in their careers or invest in new employment pathways for them. But how sure are we that there are no votes in science, or that the public wouldn't support science if it were asked? Does science illiteracy necessarily produce indifference or hostility to the work that scientists do? Daniel Greenberg, editor and publisher of *Science and Government Report*, and formerly of *Science*, thinks not. He recently told a university audience that polling regularly shows that 73 percent of the public consider the benefits of science greater than any of its baneful effects.[22]

Indeed, there is some empirical evidence that scientists may themselves be at fault for not cultivating a support base that already exists. In 1983 sociologist Jon Miller, who reports biennially on public attitudes toward science, studied 287 science policy leaders and found "a woeful lack of interest in mobilizing the 'science-attentive public.'"[23] This was partly because they were unaware of the size of this group (about thirty million, according to Miller's surveys and calculations), and because during the long postwar period from 1945 to 1983 government was willing to respond to the science elite with generous funding. On those occasions when they needed public support, the major disciplinary societies and professional associations tended to focus on their own membership. There was little or no overt effort to identify and mobilize the millions of private citizens interested in science.[24]

Indeed, for 1979 through 1981, only 5% of Miller's self-identified "science-attentive public" reported contacting a public official on a

---

[21] Hostility to science may reside in higher quarters than had previously been assumed. See Paul R. Gross and Norman Levitt, *Higher Superstition: The Academic Left and Its Quarrels with Science* (Baltimore: Johns Hopkins Press, 1994).

[22] Taken from a public lecture given at the University of California, San Diego on Oct. 4, 1994. This proportion is fairly stable. See Jon Miller, *The Public Understanding of Science and Technology 1990*, report to the National Science Foundation (Washington, D.C.: USGPO, 1992).

[23] Jon Miller, *The American People and Science Policy* (New York: Pergamon Press, 1983), pp. 41-43. Miller defines the science-attentive public as (1) having a self-defined interest in science and technology issues; (2) being knowledgeable about science and technology; and (3) engaging in a regular pattern of relevant information acquisition, i.e. reading a newspaper every day, or most of the time, reading one or more news magazines , one or more science magazines, or watching a television show like NOVA.

[24] In a compelling "textual analysis" of the testimony of university presidents from the Association of American Universities before congressional committees dealing with research funding over the period 1980-1985, Sheila Slaughter finds the same leaders-to-leaders orientation. Sheila Slaughter, "Beyond Basic Science: Research University Presidents' Narratives of Science Policy," *Science, Technology, and Human Values* 18, no. 3 (Summer 1993): pp. 278-302.

science-related matter in the previous year, and most of these contacts were on resource-related, not research-related, issues.[25] The reason for the public's inaction regarding science, Miller insists, was not lack of concern, but *lack of information as to what the science community would have had them do*. The 287 science and technology leaders polled by Miller confirmed this impression. They thought they could go it alone. Given the intense competition for federal resources in the decade ahead (and he saw this beginning in 1983), Miller warned that lack of mobilization of public support would put funding and science itself in grave danger.[26]

Miller's findings are provocative on several grounds, first because he departs from the notion that a "science attentive public" need be science literate,[27] and second because of his identification of a substantial population (19.5% of all adults) as science-interested citizens.[28] This indicates that our ideal scenario need not be so farfetched as it first appears if steps are taken to educate and mobilize this population. A second provocative element is Miller's identification of an elitist and preoccupied science leadership rendered inattentive to the broader public by decades of federal support. In his survey, only one of five of the leaders queried had attempted to inform the general public on science and technology issues, with leaders from the university sector being the *least likely* to have done so.[29]

---

[25] Miller, *The American People*, p. 132. An exception was the zeroing out of the science-education budget at NSF in 1981 by the Reagan Administration, which generated a substantial citizen protest, largely because the education community joined in. Pressure of the "mobilized public" helped, Miller says, to persuade a sufficient number of members of Congress of the value of science education, though the budget was still decimated.

[26] According to Miller's figures, federal support for basic research increased from $234 million in 1953 to $2.8 billion in 1968, declined for most of the 1970s, and reached $2.9 billion again only in 1978, and $3.1 billion in 1980.

[27] Depending on the definition, the number of Americans who meet a minimum standard of "science literacy" falls between 3 and 6 percent of the adult population. But "science literacy" may not be as important to support for science as "science appreciation" (a phrase allegedly invented by Edward Teller)."Science appreciators" would better correspond to Miller's "science attentive public." For a discussion of these issues, see Morris H. Shamos, "Science Literacy is Futile; Try Science Appreciation," *The Scientist* (Oct. 3, 1988): p. 8; and "Causes and Effects of Scientific Illiteracy Defined and Explored," an interview with James Trefil, *Chemical and Engineering News* (Mar. 14, 1994): p. 26.

[28] Miller's surveys are reported in the National Science Board's *Science and Engineering Indicators*, 1980, 1982, 1985, 1987, 1989, 1991, and 1993. His data sets are archived at the International Center for the Advancement of Science Literacy, Chicago Academy, 2001 N. Clark St., Chicago, Ill. 60614.

[29] Miller, *The American People*, p. 37.

Mobilizing Support for Science

It is not as if there are no precedents for informing and influencing a science-attentive public. Dorothy Nelkin in her book *Selling Science* reminds us that, as early as 1919 with the founding of the American Chemical Society, professional science writers were employed to describe research in language the public could understand.[30] The Scripps *Science Service* was established in 1930 to do the same, and even in their early years, the American Institute of Physics (founded in 1935) and the American Association for the Advancement of Science had wire services. When it has reason to, industry knows how to sell science and scientists. Aside from merchandising consumer products based on new technologies, industry often calls on scientists to help explain science-related issues. The chemical industry has used "advertorials" featuring scientists who are "managing chemical wastes." Westinghouse created a Campus America program in 1976 to train scientists for public debate on nuclear power. The use of scientists in public relations is not the same as building positive public relations for science (and may sometimes have the opposite effect).[31] But the "campaign mentality" does provide a model for influencing public attitudes.

Scientists are sometimes ambivalent about the press, but the press is even more ambivalent about science. There are fewer and fewer newspapers employing science writers, and the weekly science sections are disappearing. It is all but impossible to report on serious science either in the print media or on TV, not because writers are reluctant, but because, aside from health and medicine, business offices, editors, and publishers do not value science enough. Indeed, scientists might well be wary. In an article based on their study of anti-scientism among American intellectuals (see footnote 21), Norman Levitt and Paul R. Gross note that the "old respect" in which science used to be held "is being supplanted by hostile criticism . . . arising from the just and understandable desire, shared by many intellectuals, that science be democratized."[32]

Of course the extension of a science-trained work force to groups hitherto excluded from science will bring with it some risk to the habits and traditional values of the work, just as popularization may lead to

---

[30] Dorothy Nelkin, *Selling Science: How the Press Covers Science and Technology* (New York: W. H. Freeman, 1987), pp. 133-135.

[31] Ibid., p. 146.

[32] Norman Levitt and Paul R. Gross, "The Perils of Democratizing Science," *The Chronicle of Higher Education* (Oct. 5, 1994): p. B1, B2. See also Daryl E. Chubin, "Progress, Culture, and the Cleavage of Science from Society," in *Science, Technology, and Social Progress*, ed. S. L. Goldman (Bethlehem, Penn.: Lehigh University Press, 1989), pp. 177-195.

criticism and loss of prestige. But, properly understood, Levitt and Gross are as eloquent as Gerald Holton in making the case that science, in its constant battle against fanaticism and obscurantism, is a critical support for democratic society.[33]

Conclusion

Members of Congress and others are calling for a "new social compact" between science and society, one that contributes to solving the next generation of economic and social problems.[34] The COSEPUP (Committee on Science, Engineering, and Public Policy) report of the National Academy of Sciences, released in April 1995, calls for a balanced blend of research and preparation for diverse career paths in the training of future science professionals, a goal already adumbrated by study commissions of the American Chemical and the American Physical Societies.[35] And thoughtful scientists from all disciplines have nearly conceded—but as yet mainly in theory—that the "old compact" rooted in the cold war and U.S. economic hegemony, in which "science was placed in a special category above politics,"[36] cannot be revived.

No less important than the emerging shift in perceptions and expectations will be shifts in the realities that constrain change: how future federal budgets (and budget-cutting) will affect the amount, manner of dispersal, and criteria for funding of research, including the mix between strategic and untargeted (basic or curiosity-driven); how universities will select, train, and direct the next generation of science professionals into certain specialties (and not into others); and whether unrestrained access by foreign nationals to U.S. scientific training and scientific jobs will be allowed to diminish the career prospects of U.S. citizens. In short, the financial support mechanisms and the institutional rearrangements required by the "new social compact" need to be hammered out in relentless debate among all who have, or ought to have, a stake in America's scientific future.

Some readers may be tempted to ignore our perceptions and that of

---

[33] Levitt and Gross, "The Perils of Democratizing," p. B2. Gerald Holton, *Science and Anti-Science* (Cambridge, Mass.: Harvard University Press, 1994), especially his retort to Vaclav Havel in chap. 6, pp. 145-185.

[34] George E. Brown, Jr. put this in writing in his "New Ways of Looking at U.S. Science and Technology," *Physics Today* (Sept.1994): pp. 31-35; and in "Common Sense, Science, and a Balanced Budget" (presentation to the NAS, Jan. 1995).

[35] COSEPUP report, NAS, *Reshaping the Graduate Education of Scientists and Engineers* (Washington, D.C.: National Academy Press, 1995).

[36] John Deutsch, speaking as deputy secretary of the Department of Defense, at a meeting of engineering deans, Washington, D.C., Mar. 9 and 10, 1995.

our respondents if they think these don't (yet) correspond to *their* research areas, *their* students, or *their* perceptions. But we believe they do so at their peril. The fortunes of other research areas, other departments, and other students will have an impact on research and teaching in all subdisciplines, and any changes in federal policy and budgeting, even those not immediately targeted at them, will affect the way they do business. They are, in short, part of a larger system, even if they don't think of themselves that way. From this perspective, downsizing and so-called academic birth control, while appealing in the short run, can emasculate what's good about the whole system—the community. In science, as in nature, there is an ecology at work. The science community owes it to itself not to generalize from one node or perch but, rather, to raise the caliber, the productivity, and the utility of the whole enterprise.

Nor ought the science community, in our view, continue to do on an ad hoc basis those things that require a sound empiricism. Issues of careers in science need to be dealt with promptly and responsibly, consistent with the best interests of the young professionals involved and the long-term welfare of the nation as a whole. Failure to do so will make science as a career appear even more risky to those contemplating their futures than it does today. So, we end where we began, with these questions:

> *How will our nation grow the scientists it needs?*
> *How will our scientists get the work they've trained for?*
> *And dare we leave these matters to chance?*

Appendix

Appendix

Section I replicates the Career Questionnaire in full. This questionnaire was the basic tool for collecting the responses summarized in chapters 2 and 3. It alone sufficed for university respondents, but industrial scientists complained that it was too academic in its orientation, and a set of questions was added (Industry Questionnaire, Section II). Later, when graduates in the physical sciences from University of Nebraska, Carleton, and Mount Holyoke Colleges were queried, another set of questions was added (Graduate Questionnaire, Section III).

The Applicant Questionnaire for failed applicants for academic positions required a different approach, and is reproduced in full as Section IV. Responses to it are discussed in chapter 4. Section V consists of open-ended questions about education and training posed to members of the Young Scientists' Network in August 1994.

Answers to multiple-choice questions on all five questionnaires are shown, as aggregated. Answers to the open-ended questions were quoted as appropriate, in the preceding text. (The enumeration of questions below is for ease of reading.)

SECTION I
Basic Career Questionnaire and Responses

Responses to the simple closed-ended questions in the Career Questionnaire are given in tabular form. The number of respondents, N, is given for each question, with the corresponding percent of total in parentheses. In some cases, only certain respondents—only those who switched careers, for example—answered a group of questions. Hence the N is lower.

	Career[1] N	App.[2] N	Indus.[3] N	Grad.[4] N	Grad.[5] N
Respondents	85	268	68	172	204

Sex

	Career[1] N (%)	App.[2] N (%)	Indus.[3] N (%)	Grad.[4] N (%)	Grad.[5] N (%)
Respondents	83 (98)	268 (100)	68 (100)	169 (98.3)	204 (100)
Male	44 (53)	221 (82.5)	40 (59)	152 (89.9)	0 (0)
Female	39 (47)	47 (17.5)	28 (41)	17 (10.1)	204 (100)

Age

	Career[1] N (%)	App.[2] N (%)	Indus.[3] N (%)	Grad.[4] N (%)	Grad.[5] N (%)
Respondents	84 (99)	260 (97)	68 (100)	172 (100)	204 (100)
19-29	7 (8)	11 (4.2)	1 (1)	32 (18.6)	15 (7.3)
30-39	28 (33)	181 (69.6)	25 (37)	42 (24.4)	49 (24)
40-49	21 (25)	53 (20.4)	29 (43)	36 (20.9)	37 (18.1)

[1] Career Questionnaire
[2] Applicant Questionnaire
[3] Career and Industry

[4] Career and Graduate: Carleton; Nebraska
[5] Career and Graduate: Mount Holyoke

50-59	23 (27)	14 (5.4)	11 (16)	38 (22.1)	33 (16.2)
60+	5 (6)	1 (0.4)	2 (3)	24 (14)	70 (34.2)

Highest degree

	Career[1]	App.[2]	Indus.[3]	Grad.[4]	Grad.[5]
	N (%)	N (%)	N (%)	N (%)	N (%)
Respondents	84 (99)	267 (99.6)	68 (100)	170 (98.8)	203 (99.5)
B.S./B.A.	6 (7)	0 (0)	5 (7)	34 (20)	39 (19.2)
M.S./M.A.	9 (11)	0 (0)	5 (7)	41 (24.1)	54 (26.6)
M.D.	0 (0)	0 (0)	0 (0)	2 (1.2)	40 (19.7)
J.D.	0 (0)	0 (0)	0 (0)	1 (0.6)	3 (1.5)
Ph.D.	69 (82)	267 (100)	58 (85)	88 (51.8)	58 (28.6)
Other[6]	2 (2)	0 (0)	0 (0)	4 (2.4)	9 (4.4)

What year was your highest degree conferred? 19__

In what field did you earn your highest degree?

	Career[1]	App.[2]	Indus.[3]	Grad.[4]	Grad.[5]
	N (%)	N (%)	N (%)	N (%)	N (%)
Respondents	84 (99)	268 (100)	68 (100)	169 (98.3)	204 (100)
Chemistry	41 (49)	77 (28.7)	46 (67)	1 (0.6)	87 (42.6)
Physics	18 (21)	152 (56.7)	4 (6)	125 (74)	2 (1)
Biology	6 (7)	0 (0)	5 (7)	0 (0)	2 (1)
Other	19 (23)	39 (14.5)	13 (19)	43 (25.4)	113 (55.4)

If this field is different from that of your other degree(s) please indicate the other field(s):

Work history

1. In ___ years since earning your highest degree, how many salaried positions have you held?

2. Aside from the postdoc(s), how many of these have required scientific training?

	Career[1]
	N (%)
Respondents	83 (98)
All	76 (91)
Most	2 (2)
None	4 (5)
Other	1 (1)

3. Aside from the postdoc, what attracted you most to the first science-based position you were in?

4. What attracted you most to your current position?

5. What skills derived from your scientific training have proved to be the most valuable throughout your career?

[1] Career Questionnaire
[2] Applicant Questionnaire
[3] Career and Industry
[4] Career and Graduate: Carleton; Nebraska
[5] Career and Graduate: Mount Holyoke
[6] Multiple degrees listed

6. Looking back on your career, to whom (as opposed to what) do you most attribute your choice of science:

	Career[1] N (%)	Industry[3] N (%)
Respondents	83 (98)	68 (100)
Parent	25 (30)	13 (19)
Teacher/Prof.	43 (52)	40 (59)
Sibling	1 (1)	3 (4)
Other	32 (39)	17 (25)

7. What experiences listed below helped convince you that a career in science was appealing or possible: (check all that apply)

	Career[1] N (%)	Industry[3] N (%)
Respondents	84 (99)	68 (100)
Interest in nature	54 (64)	40 (59)
Magazines and books	51 (61)	32 (47)
Summer camp	7 (8)	9 (13)
Lab experiments in school	34 (40)	34 (50)
After school experiences	8 (10)	N/A
TV shows	12 (14)	8 (12)
Nothing in particular	4 (5)	5 (7)
Other	52 (62)	34 (50)

8. Earlier generations of scientists have subscribed to the view that they were "called" to science, much like others are called to the priesthood. What do you think of "calling" as an explanation for choosing science as a career?

9. If you had to consider all the influences on your choosing a career in science, what fractions would you apportion to the following: family; school; media; active recruitment by _____; long-standing, idiosyncratic interest; unconscious and unplanned; other (Total = 100%)

10. How important were each of the following in influencing your decision to accept the first position—other than postdoc—you held in science (v = very important; i = important; n = not important; d = didn't even enter my mind): salary; job security; partner/spouse wishes; geographic location; intellectual challenge; quality of coworkers; opportunity to learn; opportunity for advancement; kind of organization (e.g., academic, government, private)

Career satisfaction

11. At a minimum, satisfaction with one's career choice can be thought of as an agreement between expectations and experiences. Looking back, how well-informed were you about the commitment to a career in science? Please check all that apply below: I was . . .

	Career[1] N (%)	Industry[3] N (%)
Respondents	85 (100)	68 (100)
Very well-informed	11 (13)	6 (9)
Informed enough to be comfortable	38 (45)	32 (47)
Trusting of major professors/mentors	43 (51)	32 (47)
Confident about the fit between my skills/interests and opportunities for a career in science	58 (68)	55 (81)

Not well-informed	28	(33)	19	(28)
Too trusting of what I was told about the future	17	(20)	5	(7)
Misled by those I relied on who themselves were uninformed	2	(2)	3	(4)

Please elaborate on those you checked above:

12. In what sector have you spent most of your career: academic; federal government; private company; nonprofit; K-12 education; other (specify)

13. A career in science requires the playing of many roles. How many of the following have you done in the last six months? (check all that apply)

	Career[1] N (%)	Industry[2] N (%)
Respondents	85(100)	68(100)
Taught an undergraduate class	50 (59)	N/A
Advised a student on his/her career plans	67 (79)	N/A
Wrote a letter of recommendation for a student seeking admission to graduate school	47 (55)	N/A
Wrote a letter of recommendation for a graduate student seeking a position	20 (24)	N/A
Completed a piece of scientific work and drafted a manuscript reporting the results	49 (58)	47 (69)
Published an article in a scientific journal	41 (48)	25 (37)
Reviewed a manuscript submitted for publication to a scientific journal	39 (46)	27 (40)
Presented a paper at a research seminar or conference away from your home institution	45 (53)	32 (47)
Participated in conference on teaching in your field	34 (40)	N/A
Consulted for a company or other organization on a research or teaching matter	35 (41)	N/A
Acted as a reviewer of proposals submitted to a government agency for funding consideration	29 (34)	13 (19)
Prepared a research or teaching proposal for submission to a funding agency	37 (44)	N/A
Other	31 (36)	34 (50)

14. Which of the above were the most satisfying in terms of professional achievement, and why?

15. How would you rate your overall satisfaction with your career in science?

	Career[1] N (%)	Indus.[2] N (%)	Grad.[3] N (%)	Grad.[4] N (%)
Respondents	85(100)	68(100)	172(100)	191(93.6)
Very Satisfied	33 (39)	34 (50)	74 (43)	90 (47.1)
Satisfied enough to do it again	42 (49)	29 (43)	83(48.3)	86 (45)
Disappointed	7 (8)	4 (6)	12 (7)	12 (6.3)
Dissatisfied enough that I would pursue a different career	0 (0)	0 (0)	N/A	N/A
Other	3 (4)	1 (1)	2 (1.2)	3 (1.6)

16. Is your satisfaction with your career more a reflection on your training, your work, or a combination of both? Please explain:

17. What advice would you give to high school students and undergraduates? What would you recommend, or perhaps warn about, that you were never told?

18. How important are each of the following to your sense of satisfaction with your career? (v = very important; s = somewhat important; n = not important) ability to move up; opportunity to be autonomous, flexible, and make a contribution; feeling that my institution appreciates and cares about me; the collegiality and learning from my peers; my singleminded dedication ("keeping an eye on the prize"); other (specify)

19. How much does satisfaction with one's career depend on things outside of science, e.g., the state of the economy, national politics, or your boss's personality, as opposed to things under one's own control? Please comment in general and then with regard to your own career experience.

20. What words do you associate with, and find synonymous with, "satisfaction" as it applies to careers? (list 3-4 below)

Career Change

21. Have you experienced a career change?

	Career[1] N (%)	Industry[2] N (%)
Respondents	84 (99)	67 (99)
Yes	47 (56)	33 (49)
No	37 (44)	34 (51)

22. If no, skip the rest of this page and the next; if yes, how would you characterize the change? (check all that apply)

	Career[1] N (%)	Industry[2] N (%)
Respondents	47 (100)	33 (100)
Change in status, e.g., postdoc to continuing position	12 (26)	22 (67)
Change in sector, e.g., academic to industrial	14 (30)	12 (36)
Change in job description, e.g., research to administration	23 (49)	N/A
Change in family obligations	9 (19)	N/A
Movement out of science altogether	7 (15)	3 (9)
Other	21 (45)	11 (33)

23. For every career change, it is said there are "push" factors that hasten the move, and "pull" factors that attract one to a new opportunity. On balance, have your career changes been due more to push or to pull factors?

	Career[1] N (%)	Indus.[2] N (%)	Grad.[3] N (%)	Grad.[4] N (%)
Respondents	47 (100)	31 (94)	36 (88)	50 (76)
Push	23 (49)	17 (55)	7 (19)	4 (8)
Pull	15 (32)	8 (26)	25 (69)	41 (82)
Both	9 (19)	6 (19)	4 (11)	5 (10)

24. Please explain.

[1] Career Questionnaire
[2] Career and Industry
[3] Career and Graduate: Carleton; Nebraska
[4] Career and Graduate: Mount Holyoke

25. Was your career change in any way due to organizational barriers, i.e., your employing institutions prohibited/deterred your professional growth?

	Career[1] N (%)	Industry[2] N (%)
Respondents	46 (98)	31 (94)
No	27 (58)	20 (65)
Yes	19 (41)	11 (35)

26. Please explain.

27. Do you believe the operation of larger cultural obstacles (demographics, conservatism, racism, sexism) has inhibited upward mobility or blocked lateral moves within your organization?

	Career[1] N (%)	Industry[2] N (%)
Respondents	47(100)	33(100)
No	23 (49)	19 (58)
Yes	24 (51)	14 (42)

28. What positive developments (funding opportunities, changes in the methods/techniques/theories in your field) have influenced your career?

29. How typical do you think are your feelings, beliefs, and experiences relative to a career in science? (check all that apply)

	Career[1] N (%)	Indus.[2] N (%)	Grad.[3] N (%)	Grad.[4] N (%)
Respondents	81 (95)	68(100)	166(96.5)	187(91.7)
Typical of most scientists	17 (21)	14 (21)	30(18.1)	15 (8)
Typical of those my sex	30 (37)	13 (19)	14 (8.4)	55(29.4)
Typical of those my age	26 (32)	18 (26)	33(19.9)	59(31.6)
Typical of those in my field	28 (35)	17 (25)	N/A	N/A
Not typical at all	14 (17)	11 (16)	45(27.1)	42(22.5)
I really don't know	27 (33)	21 (31)	71(42.8)	71 (38)

30. How many years (total) do you expect to work in science?

	Career[1] N (%)	Industry[2] N (%)
Respondents	84 (99)	68 (100)
Forever, i.e., 50 years or more	38 (45)	27 (40)
Most of my career, but not all of it	35 (42)	30 (44)
Just a fraction, since I expect to do other things	3 (4)	2 (3)
Other	8 (10)	9 (13)

[1] Career Questionnaire
[2] Career and Industry
[3] Career and Graduate: Carleton; Nebraska
[4] Career and Graduate: Mount Holyoke

Social Institutions

31. In your view, should preparation for any career assure that one's skills will transfer across a variety of sectors and institutions?

	Career[1] N (%)	Industry[2] N (%)
Respondents	83 (98)	63 (93)
No	13 (16)	19 (30)
Yes	70 (84)	44 (70)

32. Please explain.

33. What does your highest degree signify to you? (check all that apply)

	Career[1] N (%)
Respondents	85(100)
Accomplishment	75 (88)
Versatility	32 (38)
Specialization	40 (47)
Attractiveness to employers	42 (49)
A "union card," or mark of legitimacy	51 (60)
A poor reflection of your skills	4 (5)
A detriment in seeking certain positions	8 (9)
Other	16 (19)

34. Some experts argue that an "academic model" dominates graduate training in science. This model values a research career in an academic setting and devalues all other scientific work and career paths. Do you agree that this model is dominant?

	Career[1] N (%)	Industry[2] N (%)
Respondents	83 (98)	65 (96)
No	16 (19)	15 (23)
Yes	67 (81)	50 (77)

35. Should such a model dominate?

	Career[1] N (%)
Respondents	79 (93)
No	72 (91)
Yes	7 (9)

36. How do market forces enter the picture?

37. If scientists and/or their employers are disturbed by the lack of opportunities for or utilization of the skills of scientists, with whom does the primary responsibility lie for fostering change? (check all that apply)

	Career[1]	Industry[2]
	N (%)	N (%)
Respondents	83 (98)	67 (99)
The scientists themselves	62 (75)	53 (79)
The universities that train them	60 (72)	38 (57)
The professors under whom one studies	37 (45)	26 (39)
The professional societies/associations that represent their interests to the rest of society	52 (63)	30 (45)
The federal government, including the R&D agencies	43 (52)	20 (30)
Business/industry	42 (51)	44 (66)
Other	6 (7)	5 (7)
Nobody: those are the vagaries of the market	6 (7)	9 (13)

38. Does the public need to be better educated about the value of science and scientists, especially their contributions to the nation's economy and work force?

	Career[1]	Industry[2]
	N (%)	N (%)
Respondents	85(100)	66 (97)
No	6 (7)	3 (5)
Yes	79 (83)	63 (95)

39. If yes, which of the following should be doing more to educate the public? (check all that apply)

	Career[1]
	N (%)
Respondents	80 (94)
Scientists	70 (87)
Local schools/teachers	59 (74)
Universities	56 (70)
Professional societies	69 (86)
Federal government	42 (53)
Industrial employers	53 (66)
Media	59 (74)
Other	7 (9)

40. Recently, magazines such as *Science, Chemical & Engineering News,* and *Physics Today* have run theme sections or special articles on "careers in science," "women in science," and "minorities in science." What are your reactions to such pieces? (check all)

	Career[1]	Industry[2]
	N (%)	N (%)
Respondents	85(100)	68(100)
I seldom read these magazines	5 (6)	15 (22)
I have read one or more such articles with interest	62 (73)	40 (59)
I pass such articles on to others for their own reading	34 (40)	17 (25)
I think such articles raise consciousness and may change perceptions about career dilemmas	59 (69)	32 (47)
I doubt such articles have much impact on behavior	21 (25)	12 (18)
Such articles are probably directed to the wrong audience	20 (24)	21 (31)
Such articles are too little, too late	11 (13)	4 (6)

41. In your view, is scientific talent being wasted in this country?

	Career[1] N (%)
Respondents	74 (87)
No	8 (11)
Yes	66 (89)

42. Please explain why you think scientists are or are not being wasted more than other professionals:

43. Does the nation need more students studying science as preparation for a career in science?

	Career[1] N (%)	Indus.[2] N (%)	Grad.[3] N (%)	Grad.[4] N (%)
Respondents	83 (98)	63 (93)	146 (84.9)	140 (68.6)
No	28 (34)	17 (27)	60 (41.1)	43 (30.7)
Yes	55 (66)	46 (73)	86 (58.9)	97 (69.3)

44. If yes, would better coordination between schools and colleges/universities increase the recruitment of students to science?

	Career[1] N (%)	Industry[2] N (%)
Respondents	55 (100)	44 (96)
No	6 (11)	6 (14)
Yes	49 (89)	38 (86)

45. If yes, what roles do higher education faculty have a direct role to play?

46. Is there a role for public policy in increasing opportunities for scientists and utilization of their skills? (check all that apply)

	Career[1] N (%)	Industry[2] N (%)
Respondents	81 (95)	65 (96)
No, that's a market issue	19 (23)	14 (22)
No, that's a scientific/technological issue	10 (12)	6 (9)
Yes, the President and Congress should do more	33 (41)	25 (38)
Yes, the R&D agencies, and especially the National Science Foundation, could be funded to do more	54 (67)	33 (51)
Yes, schools and teachers could be funded to do more	55 (68)	31 (48)
Other	15 (19)	13 (20)

47. Why or why are you not worried about the future prowess of U.S. science?

[1] Career Questionnaire
[2] Career and Industry
[3] Career and Graduate: Carleton; Nebraska
[4] Career and Graduate: Mount Holyoke

48. Do you believe there is a coming shortage of scientists and engineers in the U.S.?

	Career[1] N (%)
Respondents	71 (84)
No	38 (54)
Yes	33 (46)

49. Please comment: Do you feel our national political leaders understand how vital science is to the future of the nation?

	Career[1] N (%)
Respondents	79 (93)
No	52 (66)
Yes	27 (34)

50. Explain: Is the attention on science per se misplaced, inasmuch as creative thinking skills relate to a range of professions valuable to the well-being of the nation?

	Career[1] N (%)
Respondents	73 (86)
No	41 (56)
Yes	32 (44)

51. What have we failed to ask you that relates to a career in science—yours or the issue in general? Please tell us here:

SECTION II
Some Added Questions and Responses—Industry Questionnaire

52. Has your degree been a limiting factor in your career?

	N (%)
Respondents	67 (99)
No	59 (88)
Yes	8 (12)

53. Does the market operate any differently/better for other professions?

	N (%)
Respondents	29 (43)
No	17 (59)
Yes	12 (41)

[1] Career Questionnaire

54. Is there too much or too little attention devoted to science by government and the media, inasmuch as creative skills relate to a range of professions valuable to the well-being of the nation?

	N (%)
Respondents	56 (82)
Too little	56(100)
Too much	0 (0)

SECTION III
Some Added Questions and Responses—Graduate Questionnaire

55. I have always worked in:

	Grad.[2] N (%)	Grad.[3] N (%)
Respondents	111(64.5)	131(64.2)
Academe	62(55.8)	77 (58.8)
Industry	44(39.6)	40 (30.5)
Government	3 (2.7)	1 (0.8)
Other	2 (1.8)	13 (9.9)

56. Of the following, what were the major influences on your choice of an academic career? (check all that apply)

	Grad.[2] N (%)	Grad.[3] N (%)
Respondents	92(82.9)	100(76.3)
Family	25 (27)	42 (42)
School	45 (49)	54 (54)
Active recruitment by: _____	7 (8)	7 (7)
Unintended and unplanned choice	16 (17)	19 (19)
Other	38 (41)	24 (24)

57. Of the following, which have been instrumental in your decision to take and remain in an academic/industrial setting? (check all that apply)

	Grad.[2] N (%)	Grad.[3] N (%)
Respondents	111 (100)	116 (88.5)
Salary	44(39.6)	44 (37.9)
Job security	45(40.5)	44 (37.9)
Partner/spouse wishes	13(11.7)	18 (15.5)
Geographic location	39(35.1)	65 (56)
Opportunity to advance	42(37.8)	23 (19.8)
Quality of coworkers	53(47.7)	55 (47.4)
Opportunity to learn	84(75.7)	78 (67.2)

[2] Graduate: Carleton; Nebraska
[3] Graduate: Mount Holyoke

58. More scientists are needed at what degree level(s)?

	Grad.[1] N (%)	Grad.[2] N (%)
Respondents	85 (99)	96 (99)
Associate (2-year)	31 (36)	23 (24)
Baccalaureate	59 (69)	65 (68)
Master's	52 (61)	65 (68)
Ph.D.	27 (32)	60 (63)

59. For which sector(s) of the economy?

	Grad.[1] N (%)	Grad.[2] N (%)
Respondents	83 (96)	91 (94)
2-year colleges	17 (20)	27 (30)
4-year colleges	17 (20)	40 (44)
Universities	19 (23)	38 (42)
Industry/business	65 (78)	64 (70)
Government (federal, or specify)	27 (33)	38 (42)
K-12 school	54 (65)	63 (69)
Nonprofit	16 (19)	24 (26)

[1] Graduates: Carleton; Nebraska   [2] Graduates: Mount Holyoke

SECTION IV
The Applicant Questionnaire

Job Search Experiences

60. How long have you been looking for a position in science? (or if you found a position, how long did it take?)

61. What were your major sources of job opportunity information? (check all that apply)

	N (%)
Respondents	267 (99.6)
Ads in professional journals	257 (96.3)
Word of mouth via major professors	100 (37.5)
Word of mouth via peers	78 (29.2)
Job fairs at professional meetings	66 (24.7)
Other (specify)	187 (70)

62. Was your search confined to a certain kind of job (e.g., professor), sector (e.g., academe), or institution (e.g., liberal arts college), or did you apply for a range of positions? Please explain:

63. Looking back, there were no doubt positions you did not apply for. Was this due to (check all that apply):

	N (%)
Respondents	267 (99.6)
The position didn't interest	160 (59.9)
The institution didn't interest me	128 (47.9)
The region of the country wasn't attractive	129 (48.3)
I knew too much about the department/institution	26 (9.7)
The fit with my specialization wasn't right	195 (73)
My spouse/partner wasn't thrilled by the prospect	75 (28.1)
The opportunity was not enough of an improvement over my current situation to warrant the effort of applying	83 (31.1)
Other (describe)	43 (16.1)

64. In your most recent job search, how many in-person interviews did you get?

	N (%)
Respondents	266 (99.3)
None	67 (25.2)
One	55 (20.7)
Two or more	144 (54.1)

65. Have you completed a postdoc?

	N (%)
Respondents	266 (99.3)
No	110 (41.4)
Yes	156 (58.6)

66. If yes, how many have you had:

67. For how many years total:

68. Has your postdoc(s) helped or hindered your landing your next position? (why or why not)

69. Coming out of graduate school, what would you have done differently in searching for a position than what you did?

70. How did your major professor(s) help in your latest job search?

71. What other kinds of assistance would you have liked during this latest search?

Comments on the Search Process

72. What currently are your dominant feelings about your job search? (check one)

	N (%)
Respondents	266 (99.3)
Satisfaction with the process	31 (11.7)
Mixed emotions	129 (48.5)
Despair	70 (26.3)
Other (specify:)	55 (20.7)

73. Please explain:

What about the process disturbed you the most?

74. If you have not gotten a position for which you recently applied, to what do you attribute this (check all that apply)?

	N (%)
Respondents	264 (98.5)
The job was wired for someone else	107 (40.5)
It was not really my area	89 (33.7)
The economy and the market are such that I'm not surprised	165 (62.5)
Characteristics unrelated to competence were probably decisive (e.g. gender or ethnicity)	90 (34.1)
The position called for a track record that is not my strength (e.g., considerable federal or private research funding, reputation as an outstanding teacher)	98 (37.1)
I really don't know	65 (24.6)
Other (specify:)	2 (0.8)

75. Would you generalize about your experience, i.e., certain kinds of institutions or departments are more candid, supportive, fair, etc., than others?

76. What have you learned about your field and people in it that you did not realize until you looked for a position?

77. If you do not find a satisfactory position in a college or university, what do you think you will do with your training?

78. What would have been your second career choice during your undergraduate years?

79. Why did science win out at the time?

SECTION V
Questions to Young Scientists' Network

80. What is your field and degree level?

	N (%)
Respondents	38 (100)
Physics	22 (58)
Chemistry	6 (16)
Other	10 (26)
Ph.D.	35 (92)
Other	3 (8)

81. Had you known what the job situation would be, what would you have done differently in your graduate study?

82. What courses, apprenticeships, or training would have added value to your degree?

83. What non-science electives are you finding of value in your current job?

84. Does your strategy for what to do next include seeking another degree?

	N (%)
Respondents	38(100)
No	25 (66)
Yes	13 (34)

85. If so, which degree and field?

86. Why will you seek another degree?

About the Authors

Sheila Tobias

This is the third in the series of books Sheila Tobias has written for Research Corporation as part of a long-term research and writing assignment on neglected issues in science education. The first two, *They're not Dumb, They're Different: Stalking the Second Tier* (1990) and *Revitalizing Undergraduate Science: Why Some Things Work and Most Don't* (1992), dealt with the need to attract a wider variety of able students to undergraduate science and the barriers to reforming science programs. She is also the author of *Overcoming Math Anxiety*, first published in 1978 and reissued in 1994; *Succeed with Math: Every Student's Guide to Conquering Math Anxiety* (1987); *Breaking the Science Barrier* (with physicist Carl T. Tomizuka, 1992); and two books on defense policy and perceptions, *The People's Guide to National Defense* (1982), and *Women, Militarism, and War* (edited with Jean Bethke Elstain, 1990). Future writings include a book about in-class examinations in college-level science, and one covering the history of the second wave of feminism in America. Tobias has been an administrator at Cornell and Wesleyan Universities and a lecturer on many campuses including City College of New York, Vanderbilt, UCSD, Carleton College, Claremont Graduate School, and the University of Southern California.

Daryl E. Chubin

Since September 1993, Daryl Chubin has been division director for research, evaluation, and dissemination in the Education and Human Resources Directorate of the National Science Foundation. He began his federal service in 1986 as senior analyst and later senior associate in the Science, Education, and Transportation Program, Office of Technology Assessment (OTA), U.S. Congress. Prior to that, he taught at Georgia Tech, Penn, Cornell, and Southern Illinois at Edwardsville. He is the author of five books, including *Peerless Science: Peer Review and U.S. Science Policy* (coauthored with E. J. Hackett, 1990), and was project director for the OTA reports *Federally Funded Research: Decisions for a Decade* (1991), and *Educating Scientists and Engineers: Grade School to Grad School* (1988). Chubin is a founding member of the Society for Social Studies of Science and was elected a Fellow of the American Association for the Advancement of Science in 1990. He is also adjunct professor in the Cornell-in-Washington Program.

Kevin Aylesworth

After graduating in 1989 with a Ph.D. in experimental condensed-matter physics from the University of Nebraska, Kevin Aylesworth served as a National Research Council postdoctoral associate at the Naval Research Laboratory in Washington, D.C. He founded the Young Scientists' Network in 1990 to alert policymakers to the deteriorating job market in science. He remains active in science policy. In 1993 Aylesworth was elected for a four-year term as a general councillor of the American Physical Society. After his postdoc, he became a self-employed technical consultant. His first contract was to provide expert advice on scientific method to the lead counsel for Daubert in the 1992 Supreme Court case, *Daubert vs. Merrill Dow Pharmaceuticals*. He will be an American Physical Society Congressional Fellow in 1995-96.

Jacqueline Raphael, chief research and editorial assistant

Jacqueline Raphael is an education writer based in Tucson, Arizona. She holds a B.A. in English from Yale University and an M.F.A. in writing from the University of Arizona. She is coauthor of the forthcoming *In-class Examinations: New Theory, New Practice For the Teaching and Assessment of College-level Science* (California State University Foundation). She is also a program evaluator for the Image Processing for Teaching Project at the University of Arizona.

About Research Corporation
A foundation for the advancement of science

One of the first U.S. foundations and the only one wholly devoted to the advancement of science, Research Corporation was established in 1912 by scientist, inventor, and philanthropist Frederick Gardner Cottrell with the assistance of Charles Doolittle Walcott, Secretary of the Smithsonian Institution. Its objectives: to make inventions "more available and effective in the useful arts and manufactures," and "to provide means for the advancement and extension of technical and scientific investigation, research and experimentation . . . ."

Cottrell's inspiration—he was a physical chemist at the University of California—was to create Research Corporation to develop his invention, the electrostatic precipitator for controlling industrial air pollution, and other discoveries from universities, and devote any monies realized to grants for scholarly research. In an era before government support of science was established, Research Corporation played a crucial role in husbanding and maintaining academic research in the United States. It continues in this science support mission down to the present day.

Research Corporation awards support scientific inquiry in physics, chemistry, and astronomy at public and private undergraduate institutions (Cottrell College Science Awards); assist beginning university faculty members wishing to excel in *both* research and teaching (Cottrell Scholars Awards); and help midcareer scientists in establishing new research programs (Research Opportunity Awards). Other initiatives improve high school science education by giving teachers opportunities to do summer research at local colleges and universities (Partners In Science), and fund promising research and prizes not falling under other programs (General Awards).

Applications from college and university scientists are reviewed by referees suggested by applicants and supplemented, as appropriate, by the foundation. A final reading of applications and recommendations for approval or denial are given by an advisory committee of academic scientists. Research Corporation awards are supported by its endowment created through Dr. Cottrell's gift of patent rights, and by donations from other academic scientists, foundations, industrial companies, and individuals wishing to advance science.

Rethinking Science as a Career: Perceptions and Realities in the Physical Sciences is the third in a series aimed at advancing research and education in the physical sciences. Both causes are served by promoting wise use of trained specialists, and science literacy for all students. The foundation will consider for publication other papers broadly relevant to its chartered objectives. Research Corporation's office is located at 101 North Wilmot Road, Suite 250, Tucson, Arizona 85711-3332.

Index

Index